GO SOLO
How to Quit the Job You Hate and Start a Small Business You Love!

Now is Your time!
Kelsey H

KELSEY HUMPHREYS
timetogosolo.com

Copyright © 2014 Kelsey Humphreys
All rights reserved.

No part of this publication may be reproduced, distributed, or transmitted in any form or by any means, including photocopying, recording, or other electronic or mechanical methods, without the prior written permission of the publisher, except in the case of brief quotations embodied in reviews and certain other non-commercial uses permitted by copyright law.

ISBN-13: 978-1502458278
ISBN-10: 1502458276

Many thanks first to my ever-supportive husband for, well, supporting me, yet again. Thank you Chloe for being really cute on Mommy's tough days. Thank you to my parents who enthusiastically read my rough draft in its entirety, especially my entrepreneur and author Dad (Dr. Owen Weston)!

Additional thanks to all of my family, my book-publishing gurus Chandler Bolt, James Roper and Tyler Wagner, my pre-solo mentors Eric Joiner, Rusty Duncan, Doug Farthing and Bobbie Earles, and to Dallas and Robyn Jones for believing in me and providing my Big Break Out Opportunity.

Biggest thank you of all to my earliest cheerleaders and readers Allison Niebes-Davis, Sara Spradling, Y.O.U.R. (Dr. Roger Lane), Jaron Jedlicka, Lauren Herrell, Abbie Unger, all the LaunchOut Launchers, Sami Kirkendall, and Kristin Blazy.

TABLE OF CONTENTS

Introduction
    Stuck in the 9-to-5 Wilderness   1

Part 1. FIND YOUR PASSION
(You're Going to Need It)
1. Don't Buy the "Normal" Lie   9
2. How to Choose the Right Passion and Peak for You   19
3. Why Go Solo at All?   31

Part 2. FOCUS YOUR EFFORTS
4. Learn Before You Launch   39
    Make the Most of Your Final Employed Days
5. Help Your Big Breakout Opportunity Find You   49
6. Set Your Pace For Success   59

Part 3. FULFILL YOUR PURPOSE
7. Prepare for Your Departure   71
8. Rethink Your Revenue Streams and Save that Date!   79
9. Branding Your Business for Success   87
10. Yes, You Can Start Right Now   101
11. How to Stay Hungry (After You're Bringing in the Bacon)   111

Conclusion
    Now is Your Time   123

Action Guide   i

"May your dreams be larger than mountains and may you have the courage to scale their summits."

Harley King

INTRODUCTION
Stuck in the 9-to-5 Wilderness

> "Don't become a wandering generality.
> Be a meaningful specific."
> Zig Ziglar

Imagine with me a glorious mountaintop; your personal peak. It is a beautiful place. A place where you love your day-to-day life. A place where you are contributing your unique gifts to the world. A place where you are doing work that matters. A place where your efforts directly affect your income, and you are making plenty of income! A place where you can focus on your priorities and manage your own schedule. A place where all of your goals are clearly defined and within reach. A place where your dreams are coming true. A place where you are your absolute best self. A place of freedom. A place where finally, you work and live on your own terms. It's real, it's breath taking, and it's sitting there, just waiting for you.

Are you headed there? Are you close enough to even see the mountain range of dreams fulfilled? Or have you found yourself in a dry, desolate, itchy-sand-as-far-as-you-can-see wasteland? Even worse, do you feel trapped there? Are you stuck, as if pinned to a cactus, left to rot in the 9-to-5 sun, wasting your passions, talents, potential and life's most precious commodity, your time?

It's hip right now to quote Tolkien and say, *"Not all who wander are lost."* Many creative, adventurous, entrepreneurial types have taken this up as a mantra of sorts. I have a few theories as to why, but I think the main reason is the need to escape. **The idea of traveling, reading great books, and getting "off the grid" is so appealing**

because day-to-day life has become so suffocating. Wandering is better than facing the fact that we are living life on someone else's terms, cornered in a life we don't love. Some may cling to that quote because they feel they are simply too young to have to worry about a "life plan" or long-term goals. Some believe that talent alone ensures them an extraordinary life, no planning required. Perhaps being a go-getter, a do-er, and a planner has become a bit "square." No hip, innovative, creative young-ish person wants to do or be anything that might be "square." Am I right?

Tolkien's statement is definitely true, and very warm and fuzzy, but my concern is that many feel as if wandering isn't a choice. They see no way out; they feel "stuck" in the depths of the "normal job" valley. Those who are distracting themselves from the reality of their soul-sucking job will wake up years from now frustrated, confused, and disappointed. I see many talented people who I fear will look back and realize all that wandering was just wasting time. **You see, you can't reach your peak by wandering there. One does not wander into greatness. You cannot simply hope to eventually do meaningful work on your own terms.** Wishing to someday control your schedule and fuel your passions will not get you there. Even if your goal were to *literally* wander the earth, you would have to plan to do so! You would have to quit your job, find money to support the journey, get a map, and a way of finding tools, shelter and supplies.

Well, guess what? That's what this book is going to do. Solo is designed to help you create your map, gather your tools and supplies, and get the heck outta Dodge! First, you'll find and clarify your passions — what itching dreams have you been trying to ignore? What talents, gifts and strengths are collecting dust in the corner? Trust me, you will need passion to keep you climbing along your solopreneurial path. Next, you'll focus your efforts to better prepare you to start your own business. Personal branding and marketing will make it easier for you to find your ideal clients and customers, and easier for them to find you. The sooner they do, the sooner you start your climb! Lastly, we'll cover fulfilling your unique purpose — launching your business that impacts the world and allows you to live the passion-filled life you always imagined for yourself.

Hi, My Name is Kelsey, and I am a Recovering Wanderer

Many friends and family members didn't get why I got a graphic design degree since I was such a people person. I wanted to be a pop star or Broadway star, and loved to ham it up on stages of any kind. To be honest, looking back, it's a bit baffling to me as well. In my senior year of high school I realized that I enjoyed design, was good at it, and it would pay an actual salary — something singing professionally *might* never do. I was a teenager, and I knew everything. Didn't you guys know everything as a teenager too? What a great time of life. I didn't need a music degree to become a famous singer-songwriter, no training or classes for me! Can you imagine what my poor parents must have thought when I told them I'd found a more serious degree — art?! How reassured they must have felt when they saw that my security-net-degree included classes like "Art History" and "Drawing 101."

I wandered in and out of my career. After college, I immediately got a design job to start saving money for my wedding. After the wedding, though, I was able to start dreaming again, and so I started pursuing my music. However, as I'll explain later, I eventually put that dream away and focused on my advertising career. Since I was so restless as a designer, I forced myself to become more of a marketer and strategic thinker, and suddenly work became more fun. Eventually I was very happy in what was really my dream design job. Note, I called it my dream *design* job, not my *dream job*. Being on pitch teams and leading presentations got me on a stage of sorts, where I was able to perform under pressure. Still, as Associate Creative Director at one of the biggest and best agencies in Oklahoma, a job I enjoyed and did well, I was restless. **I felt like I was meant to be doing something else, something more.** I felt listless and anxious, so I started to prepare for my journey, which eventually led to starting my own business with an international first client. I didn't wander for long and you don't have to either.

If you're stuck in a job you hate, you're wandering. If you're staying in a job you enjoy when your heart is telling you to quit, you're wandering. If you live for the weekends — wandering. If you've failed at your last couple ventures, so you've given up, ignoring that next big idea gnawing at you — wandering. If you have huge, amazing ideas but are letting fear keep you from pursuing them — guilty! If you have gifts that you've let collect dust in the corner. If you feel the tug at your heart to do more meaningful work. If you're waiting for that leadership position... If you're waiting for your boss to give you a promotion... waiting for your product, idea, or your very self to be "ready" or for the conditions to be perfect before you start... if you think you have no gifts, that your gifts are not enough, or that you are not worthy of a passion-filled life—you are wandering.

You were created for more than listless roaming. You can make a difference in this world while also achieving success and freedom. By the end of this book, you'll have already started to break free. You will enjoy passion-filled days and goals and plans that take you closer to living life on your own terms. Don't wait until *someone else* musters the guts to land that client that would have been a perfect first client for *you*. Don't wait until *someone else* launches a product that you thought of two years ago! Don't wait until you have too many obligations and responsibilities. Today, with this book, you stop wandering and start walking towards your peak. Aren't you excited? Can you smell the fresh air? Can you see the peaks on the horizon? Let's get started!

Part 1. FIND YOUR PASSION
(You're Going to Need It)

1

Don't Buy the "Normal" Lie

We ask ourselves, Who am I to be brilliant, gorgeous, talented, and fabulous? Actually, who are you not to be? You are a child of God. Your playing small does not serve the world. There is nothing enlightened about shrinking so that other people will not feel insecure around you. We are all meant to shine, as children do. We were born to make manifest the glory of God that is within us. It is not just in some of us; it is in everyone and as we let our own light shine, we unconsciously give others permission to do the same. As we are liberated from our own fear, our presence automatically liberates others.

Marianne Williamson

James is a smart, funny guy who works for one of the largest oil and gas companies in America. He majored in energy management because he was told he was a "good fit" and what bright-eyed, straight-A, fraternity member doesn't want to be a good fit in one of the largest paying industries? Fast forward to a few years out of college. Newly married, James is secure in a high-paying job where he basically pushes paper all day. Pretty easy. Even better, he has an assistant, an amazing office with a view, the best benefits package known to man, access to a world class fitness center, a company credit card, and even an enviable amount of vacation days. James doesn't hate his job, per se, but in the back of his mind is a gnawing, nagging ache for a dream long since pushed aside. He is a put-together, well-dressed, has-it-all wanderer. Will he wake up in his 60s realizing he spent his most creative and energetic years pushing paper around?

Lucy is a tall, thin dancer who ended up as an accountant at a creative firm. Because majoring in dance was the silliest thing her parents could imagine spending 50 grand on, she majored in accounting. She has a knack for numbers and is good at her job. Extremely good, actually. She also makes decent money and gets to work at a "cool place." Yet, every day she longs for 5 p.m. She lives for weekends. She lives for her Zumba class and her hip-hop class and for the measly vacation time she gets. It's not practical to dance for a living, so she wanders each day in order to keep her paycheck.

Ben is the embodiment of the computer programmer stereotype. He loves programming in his very core like only a true, proud nerd can. He is a techy dreamer and owns about 30 domain names. He has more than three LLCs registered to his home address, but none of them has taken off enough for him to quit his day job. He has launched two different app ideas that both flopped. Ben has a big, huge, earth-shattering new idea that keeps him up at night but he's not going to go after it this time. He's finally given up, as his mom, best buddy, co-worker and girlfriend urged him to do. He'd rather wander with the rest of his contemporaries then keep failing again and again.

Sally is a natural writer. She has filled hundreds of journals in her life, and actually kept up one of her blogs for over four years. But, then Sally got married and got a job at her church. She feels like she "ought to" do the work that she's doing because the church needs help. At home, she wrangles two kids and tries her best to manage the household like a true "Proverbs 31 woman." Sally hasn't picked up the proverbial pen in two years. She doesn't mean to wander, she has a family to take care of after all, but when she finally picks up her pen again, *if* she does — will she realize she could have been writing all along?

Ginger is a brainiac who has invented a product that she knows without a doubt will change people's lives with its daily use. However, the product isn't "perfect" yet. Though she knows it's finished and ready for release, but she thinks the whole product might really wow investors more if she changes the color. She's currently staring at swatches trying to decide. Perfectionism is a cousin of procrastination and procrastination is one of the most common valleys wanderers get stuck in.

Sam is a talented designer, and has always had a knack for problem solving. He always knew he wanted to work in art. He works at a cool place, enjoys his work most of the time, and spends his free time designing or drawing or taking photographs. Although his job offers resources for career planning and advancement, he doesn't want to take on more responsibility. He hasn't really thought about where he wants to go with his career or how he'll get there. The whole process seems lame and pointless. Plus, he has his first kid on the way, so for now, he just wants to keep his job and hopefully get a raise every year.

The most heartbreaking example is Jane, who believes she has no gifts. She has always been "super ordinary" — not really a leader, not a dancer or singer. Since she believes she has nothing to give, she also believes she is just one of those people who has to stay in a "normal job" until she either marries, stays home with her kids, or eventually retires.

Chosen

First and foremost, you need to understand that you were created to be more than a wanderer. You were not created to "be normal." You were not chosen to sit in a "normal" job, like "normal" people. Who decides the standard for normal, anyway? Our parents? The neighbors our parents are trying to keep up with? The media? The Man? Our friends? Why do we "play small?" Why do we try to stuff down our deepest passions? Why are we so quick to dismiss childhood dreams? Why do we fight or make excuses for how we are wired? Every person has unique gifts and specific dreams given to them and only them. Even if your goal is to do something someone has seemingly already done, for example, quitting your job and switching to full-time freelancing. Sure, it's been done before, but no one can write, design, edit, photograph, manage, or consult exactly like you can. Maybe you're arguing that your style is exactly like someone else's. First, it isn't. Second, even if very close, you have an entirely different circle of influence than that other person. Your reach, however small, no matter who it includes, is your reach and no one else's. Whatever your talents, you were specifically given those talents by God. (You may prefer to think they came from the Universe or Great Spirit in the sky, etc. I believe in God; therefore, I will write as such).

It's really quite weighty when you stop and think about it. He could have given that illustration gift, heart for others, or analytical genius to anyone under the sun, and **out of billions of people, He chose *you*.** You were chosen to have your quirky personality, your giant dreams, and your goals. You have a one-of-a-kind heart and a one-of-a-kind brain with specific styles and unique ideas. Barring some freaky government-cloning project no one knows about yet, there is no duplicate of you on the earth, and thus no exact duplicate of your gifts. **With those gifts, whatever they are, come a responsibility! Whatever your gifts are, the world needs them. You have an obligation to the rest of us to share them!**

"But I'm Not Talented"

Now there is a lie that just ticks me off. Hearing that sentence from people is one of the reasons I decided I had to write this book. One of my dearest friends since high school has always claimed she wasn't very talented. She had skills, sure, but she wasn't a dreamer, an artist or a genius. She didn't have obvious gifts, and wasn't especially driven. After college, she joined a wickless candle multi-level sales company. Today she has over 500 people under her leadership and makes so much selling candles that she quit her full time job! She has always been organized, empathetic, loyal, caring, and articulate. She found something she loves that fits her personality perfectly. She now speaks at the company conventions on both the local and national level! This is someone without gifts? If you claim to have no gifts, maybe you are being falsely modest, in which case stop it. That's silly. More likely, you haven't taken the time to stop and truly evaluate yourself.

Another friend of mine also claimed she wasn't really gifted and she would follow up with, "Well, I guess I write, but I'm just a blogger." At the time of this writing, she has been blogging on the same blog for over *six years*. What twenty-something do you know who has kept up *any one thing* for six years? I can only think of a handful! Plus, she has over 1000 readers and makes her living through selling ad space and other products through her blog. I assured her, "Um, yes, you most definitely *do* write and that most certainly *is* a gift!

A different example is an executive friend of mine who still claims he has no real gifts even though he's worked his way up to one of the highest positions in his company. He leads others and handles enormous responsibility every day. **Gifts and talents don't always come from the right side of the brain.** Heard of Bill Gates? I don't think he paints in his free time. Many people either haven't stopped to evaluate their strengths or don't see value in their particular gifts. Many more still don't know how they can apply their gifts in a way that helps them contribute to the world. This book can help with that.

Why Passion?

Anyone who achieves real success as a solopreneur loves what they do. Working for yourself is not easy. There have been times that I have thought, "Forget it, I'll just get a 'regular job.'" I would be shocked to find an entrepreneur who hasn't said that — or given up and done it — throughout their solo career. Staying in the corporate grind is both safer and easier. There will be so many challenges to come your way, what's to keep you from giving up? The desire for freedom alone won't be enough. Passion for the work itself, and more importantly the people you are working for, will keep you climbing when things get rough. Realizing that you're leaving a mark on the world, rather than filling a seat in the workplace, is a powerful thing. That's because making a contribution to the world is something we all long to do in some way.

But What About Volunteering?

You may be asking, "Can't I just make money and find fulfillment outside of my work?" Bob Goff addresses this in his wonderful book *Love Does*. He explains how he uses his work as "fund raising" for his passions; it's an interesting concept. However, he has been in his career for years. I urge you to think long and hard about what that would mean for you today. Forty hours a week of fundraising in order to have weeknights and Saturdays of fulfillment sounds pretty exhausting. On the other hand, if you can streamline a job you don't love to bring in more money in less hours per week, thus freeing up the other hours for your true calling, the concept sounds awesome. But, how many people do you know who have managed to condense their job or business into only a few hours a week? How long did they have to work at it to get to that point? **It's pretty unlikely for most to ever get there, which is why I'd rather focus on how you can instead find or create a business plan that lines up with your true passions, allowing you to give your gifts to the world.**

Shouldland

For the same reasons people wonder why I chose an art degree, I did not fit in in the school of art. Imagine the stereotypical art class at a large public university. That was indeed what most of my classes looked like. Greasy, skinny kids, some wearing heavy eye make up, almost all wearing Converse. Or rope sandals. Only about half wore deodorant. There were paint-stained fingers and a lot of black. Then there was me, the blonde, driven, overly-peppy sorority girl. I annoyed the other students and even the professors. I got a second ear piercing in one ear to try and blend in a bit more. I thought maybe it'd work like a rad tattoo. It didn't.

In my career, I continued to be a bit of a misfit. My first job was as a graphic designer at a public relations firm. Though I did well at my position, it was a communications firm, and the design department was the ugly, misfit step child. I related more with the young account execs than I did the other designers, but didn't fit in with their side of the office either.

When I did finally work my way to ACD, many days I felt alone. I was still perceived as a creative by the executive and account teams, but no longer fit in with the creatives I was leading. **I like to think if one doesn't fit anywhere, maybe it is their time to stand out.** I have always been a hybrid, which brought me to where I am now. Who knows what would have happened if I had tried to stuff some parts of myself down and fit in to what an art student *should* be like. If I'd dropped deodorant, dyed my hair black and become a cynic, would I have landed that first job? Definitely not. If I had switched to the account side of things because a people person like me *should* be in a communications position, would I have had the creative inspiration to ever write this book? Probably not.

Perhaps you don't hate your job, but your days feel forced, like you're trying to force your creative self to color between the corporate lines. Maybe you're trying to push your way into a management role — because advancement is what we all should want — when you're happiest doing the actual work itself. Maybe you got a degree or started a career in something you're *good at* but you don't really *enjoy*. It's a muddy place where many get bogged down:

"I should love my well-paying job."

"Other people would kill to get paid to do this, I should be happy."

"I should love running this company."

Do you want to wake up at 40 and realize you have been squeezing your square self in a round hole for 20 years? That's gonna hurt. Shouldland is filled with quicksand and many a wanderer has gotten stuck there. Avoid it at all costs.

Many times throughout this book, I will encourage you to stop and reflect. I have included some swanky worksheets at the end of the book to help you with the process. So many painful course corrections could be avoided by simply stopping and truly evaluating one's self, surroundings, and goals. As a first step to defining your purpose, take some time to think through the six questions to find your passion on page ii. Don't just think about skills, consider personality traits too. The world needs your best you, so let's first stop and think through who you are! Next, we'll look closely about what it really means to you to "make it" as a solopreneur.

2

How to Choose the Right Passion and Peak for You

> You have brains in your head. You have feet in your shoes.
> You can steer yourself in any direction you choose.
> *Dr. Seuss*

Your Peak

When you think about your personal peak, your dream life of self-employment, what does it look like? What does it *really* mean for you to work for yourself? It could be becoming a *New York Times* bestselling author, opening a brick and mortar shop, having an online business empire, finally launching your product into the marketplace, or becoming a full-time freelancer. What exactly does that entail within your vision of success? Write it out, and write out everything that goes with it. For example, that may mean doing one service that you enjoy and nothing else, or it may mean collaborating with other freelancers. That may mean leading a talented virtual team, making six figures a year, a long list of clients, more pressure to keep you energized, and power suits. Or it may mean you have a small services list and work most days from your lake house in your pajamas. There is no wrong answer, just write out as much as you can think of.

If you don't write it down, you are not walking or climbing, you're wandering. In his book, *48 Days to Work You Love,* Dan Miller writes that only eight percent of the population makes goals and only three percent write them down. This is amazing to me! Dr. Gail Matthews, a psychology professor at Dominican University in California, did a study that concluded you are 42 percent more likely to achieve your goals just by writing them down. What a small investment with such a huge return! Wanderers read the book and dream about the contents; climbers read the book and do what it says! They eat the spinach! ...we'll talk about spinach in Chapter 7.

The Climb

Okay, once you've written everything out because you're an awesome doer and that's how you roll, it's time to think about what *the climb* looks like. **This is where so many miss the mark.** This part of starting the journey is what will keep you from ending up in the wrong place in a few years, disappointed and confused.

You've probably heard of the "10,000 Hour Rule." In his book, *Outliers: The Story of Success*, Malcolm Gladwell explains success in any field is due to practicing a specific task for 10,000 hours or more. That's the majority of the climb; practicing, growing, trying, trying and trying again. A common trait among both mega millionaires and successful solopreneurs is that they love what they do, but because they love it, another common trait is that they spend many hours on their work, especially when they are just getting started.

You now know that growing up I dreamed of becoming a famous singer — either as a singer/songwriter or on Broadway. As I got older, I realized Broadway was out of the question because I was not a "triple threat." Anyone who has seen me try to dance can attest to that. Writing came naturally to me and I plunked out chords well enough to keep up with my youth group worship band, which means I plunked poorly. Still, during college, I released an album to family and friends, and after graduation, I released an album for real: iTunes, CD release concert, some college radio airplay, the whole shebang. I would watch the Grammy's and envision myself up there on the TV, singing and playing my hot pink keyboard. But, you know what the *reality* of that dream was? It was night after night playing in small coffee shops, restaurants, and bars. It was hours and hours at the piano. I realized I didn't even *like* playing piano during my shows. I also noted that I hardly practiced and didn't enjoy practicing, while the talented musicians around me could do nothing but play for hours and hours.

What I truly loved was being on stage and encouraging people. I loved making the crowd laugh in between songs. I prayed before each show that people would leave feeling better than when they walked in. I loved marketing myself and designing the artwork; graphic design was my trusty "fallback degree" after all. Do you see where I am going with this? I had my sights set on a peak that was comprised of a climb I hated. This is so important. This is the big mistake to avoid. **So many set their sights set on a peak that is comprised of a climb they won't enjoy.**

The day-to-day life of an aspiring musician was not fun to me. And guess what? That's what I would have been for 10 to 15 years, *aspiring!* Thinking about the climb ahead of time can spare you the hassle of trying to figure out how to remove your album from iTunes five years later.

If you want to become a *New York Times* best selling author, you will have to sit and write every single day. You will have to share your writing with editors and revise, revise, and revise again. You will have to promote your book through book tours and speaking engagements. You will have to write more than one entire book (probably). You will have to open yourself up to criticism and share your heart and soul with the world. Does all of that sound like a party? Then great! Start climbing!

Research, Research, Research Some More

We are talking about quitting your job and starting a new life, right? Let's not take unnecessary risks. One key to choosing the right peak is to research that peak. There is no excuse today not to find a ton of information about your ideal solo career. What if you're not sure what daily life really looks like to go from where you are to Bestselling Author, for example? Time to find one and ask! Even if you *think* you know, asking a seasoned climber is still a good idea. Read some books or blogs from people who have traveled your trek already. People love to be asked for advice, so most will likely take a few minutes and tell you their story. However, make sure to ask for the nitty gritty details, not the glamorous, Instagram-filtered version.

Whatever Solo Success Means To You

I know a couple of men are passionate about making money. Not just excited about it, but truly passionate. Their goal is to build wealth and be able to invest in other people's dreams. Note that these guys are not passionate about *becoming wealthy*, they are passionate about investing and growing funds. It may sound shallow, as if it could never be truly fulfilling, but some people have a gift and a passion for managing money. Their big picture also includes giving massive amounts to charities or funding whole nonprofits with the money they manage. I give this example to show that everyone's dream is different and no dream is wrong or right. Not all peaks include wealth and promotion, but it's okay if yours does. It's also okay if part of your solopreneurial dream is to join the tiny house movement, get rid of all of your possessions, and help educate the world about living small.

Many women end up staying home because it makes financial sense, or because they can't find acceptable childcare. If a mother longs to build a business slowly now and then full time when her kiddos head off to school, what can she start today in order to prepare? **Once anyone, in any field, on any level of the proverbial ladder, stops to *really* picture what his or her ideal peak — and climb — is, then they can make a plan to get there.**

It is important to take the time to think this through honestly and be careful of ending up in Shouldland again. I have come across many creative types who say what they *think* they want — what they *should* want — to own their own creative agency someday. Yet in reality, they don't enjoy strategy or planning, can't write a marketing plan to save their life, and during presentations they fumble over themselves and sweat like a banshee (Do banshees sweat? It sounded good). They also don't want to lead others, managing finances, or wear the many other hats an entrepreneur has to wear. So actually, no, they don't want to have their own shop after all.

Once you've gotten a very clear picture of what your journey looks like, you may still be unsure if you'll truly love the climb. After all, how can you really know ahead of time since you've never experienced it? Some argue that you can never really know until you actually go and try it. Even though there will always be some unknowns before we actually go and do something, I believe we can at least get ourselves a lot closer to our ideal climb. Self-assessment can save us from so many course corrections. One of the things that kills me most about wanderers is that if they would just stop and take a moment to reflect every so often, it would change their life!

Assess Yourself

Before I started writing this book, I had to do some serious assessing. I realized that owning my own advertising agency was close, but not actually the right peak for me. Frustrated, I decided it was time to really figure my crap out. Luckily, having a newborn means there is a lot of time sitting and thinking to yourself, trying to stay awake in order to feed this little human who needs to eat every hour on the hour. Here is what I thought through. *What are the common aspects of everything I have tried so far? What is the thread that ties music/performing, design/art direction, and advertising/agency owner together? Which parts am I a total rock star at? Which parts do I suck at? Which parts are the most fulfilling to me? Which parts do I completely hate?* A new picture slowly came into view that combined my existing business, this book, helping others and all my other passions into one. Again, be brutally honest with yourself. If you need help, ask these questions to the people who know you best. I have always found my mom to be brutally honest, and almost always right. Perhaps yours is too (Thanks Mom!). The perspective of a spouse, a best friend, or a trusted leader may also be helpful.

Assess Your Time and Interests

Another key question to ask yourself is, *"What do I already do?"* Aside from fear and laziness, we make time for what we really want to do. What I actually loved became clearer when I looked at what I truly spent my time doing. When I was trying to "make it" as a singer/songwriter, instead of spending hours and hours perfecting my craft, I spent the majority of the time marketing myself. I was constantly designing and redesigning my site, album artwork, and this thing called a MySpace page. I was promoting online and networking. I was singing a little during the week, but I was mostly blogging and making funny videos. *Those things do not a famous pop star make.*

In my advertising career, I came back to books and blogs about entrepreneurship and leadership time and time again. What books and blogs do you read? What can you get sucked into until 2 a.m.? If you get sucked into cake decorating tips and tricks for hours on Pinterest, DVR every baking related show on Food Network and spend your weekends baking, maybe you're supposed to be a cake decorator! Why do we so quickly discount the things we love deeply as "just a hobby?"

Time assessment can be a bit tricky because you may spend all of your time away from work doing a hobby. Is your hobby something you could make money from? Would that be more fulfilling? Or are you using your hobby as a placeholder for what you really want to be doing because you're afraid to start?

I know I put off starting this book because I was afraid. Afraid of failure, afraid of starting yet another climb to what again might be the wrong peak. If you are watching TV or making model airplanes because you're afraid to sit and create, stop it! That's wandering, and do you want to wake up in a year with two more airplanes or an empty DVR, only to realize it's another year wasted? Another year you could have been working towards your dreams but instead let your fears stop you?

If you truly don't have time for your dreams because of your job or responsibilities, you will have to be more detailed with your audit. You are still making time for the parts of your job you like best, and putting off the things, you like least. We tend to like best the things that we do well, so picking apart your day, week and month at your job will help you answer the question.

Assess Your Desires

Another great question to ask yourself is, "What do I want to be remembered for?" Brendon Burchard writes in his books that it will all come down to three questions: *Did I live? Did I love? Did I matter?* Purpose goes beyond wanting to work for yourself. Purpose lies deeper than your skills passions, and goals. Try sitting down and writing your own obituary. It is a weird, enlightening exercise. Yes, you want to be remembered as great in your craft, but you'll realize it is so much more important to be remembered for the impact you had on others. *How did you help friends? How did you give back to your community? How did you show your love to loved ones? At the same time that you do this exercise, stop to think if you died today, what would you regret not doing?*

To go even deeper into this exercise, because writing your own obituary isn't deep enough, think about why you enjoy certain things. Danielle LaPorte has an entire platform of books and programs based on this subject and it is a deep one. She explains that our culture tends to do goal setting backwards, focusing on an achievement, when what we really want is the feeling that achievement offers us. If you have a goal of having 100,000 Twitter followers, for example, you may want to feel connected, respected, credible, famous, popular, or loved. It's not about the Twitter followers, it's about how reaching those people feels to you. For me, 100,000 Twitter followers would make me feel respected and credible. That many followers may make you feel connected or influential. Each person is different, will have different goals, and different feelings associated with their goals. Again, don't get trapped in Shouldland, believing you want what you're *supposed* to want or *supposed* to feel about that desire. If you love performing, it may be the adrenaline of feeling alive, or the feeling of release and creative expression. *All true answers are right answers.* Once you realize the feelings that you're after, you can start to find small ways to feel those things each day. For example, if the Twitter followers made your feel connected, and connection is important to you, you can put aside a few minutes each day to call a loved one or send a letter. If you love the rush of creative release when performing, you could start writing or posting videos each day, instead of limiting that feeling to just the stage. This is a deep topic but at least keeping it in mind as you go through your self-assessments will help you find the most honest answers to these questions. It will also greatly impact your overall journey.

Success Takes Focus

When you sow passion into a dream, you will reap passion for that dream. Driven, entrepreneurial dreamer types tend to sometimes resemble the dogs in the Pixar movie Up. If you haven't seen the movie you should probably put down this book, stop everything, and watch it (Grab some tissues). In the movie, a group of dogs would be totally focused on something and then *"Squirrel!"* Let me explain how this applies to us dreamers.

I do not watch music reality shows anymore, other than the *Sing Off*, which I love and totally nerd out over. Who doesn't love Ben Folds and a cappella? That's right, no one. I stopped watching *American Idol* and the like because watching those shows put fuel on a fire that I don't need to relight. Just recently I started jamming out to Broadway musicals in the car and still, even with all my fiery passion for this book, it took everything in me not to drive straight to New York, sign up for dance classes, and search for audition postings. I can't let myself listen to those tunes often. It may sound sad but I have to remind myself — I put out that fire for a reason. I do not want to spend my thirties learning to dance and standing in audition lines all day every day with younger, more talented, better-trained starlets. Can I sing as a hobby or somehow incorporate music into my big life picture? Yes, and I plan to, but making dreams a reality takes focus. Climbing to the top without slipping off a ledge or breaking a limb along the way takes focus. Finding solo success — versus living paycheck to paycheck! — takes focus. Aside from using lesser passions to help pay the bills as you get started, try not to fuel too many fires.

After having gone through the assessments in this book you should be able to clearly remind yourself that though that peak is one you'll always admire, that particular day-to-day climb is not for you. Once you find a climb that is truly fulfilling, it will be easier to enjoy old passions as hobbies, because you'll already be on a rewarding climb. You won't need to entertain "what if I had" anymore.

I hope that you've picked up from this chapter that **as much as you're choosing a destination, you're really choosing a journey.** Take some time to answer the questions on pages iv – viii to help you choose the *right* climb. Part of choosing the right business for you is to focus in on why - why bother going out on your own at all? Let's dive into your why in the next chapter!

3

Why Go Solo at All?

> "Far and away the best prize that life offers is the chance to work hard at work worth doing."
> *Theodore Roosevelt*

Imagine struggling alone up the face of the mountain. Now instead, imagine walking with a giant group of people. You're all walking in step and the crazy guy in the back starts a song. Now you're all singing and marching in time together. At night, you light huge fires and drink frothy beer out of metal tins. Doesn't that sound better than just you, the wind, and your tiny cot, alone on a cliff with wolves howling close by? Okay, dramatic illustration, but you get the idea.

There are some popular ideas out right now about making smart money so you can travel the world and live a luxurious life. The goal is to live like a millionaire without having to kill yourself earning the millions. Or the goal is to make tons of passive income online using easy systems and hardly think about your work at all. There is nothing wrong with living like a millionaire, or passive income. However, I don't believe living a life of leisure is the same as living a life of fulfillment. I think humans are designed to work. I think we have a deep need to contribute. Vacations and adventures are fun, and I plan to have more of both each passing year. But, more than that, I plan to feel the happy full-ness that comes from meaningful work; work that matters to me; work that results in emails from strangers saying "thank you."

In his book *Drive: The Surprising Truth About What Motivates Us*, Daniel H. Pink explained that years of research showed one of our three basic needs to feel fulfilled in work and life is purpose. People want to be part of something that is bigger than they are. When you were writing out your obituary, creepy as it was, you probably realized that whatever your peak, it won't be meaningful if it doesn't involve others. To get out of bed on the tough days and to stay focused for the long haul, a large part of your life's work or mission has to be bigger than yourself.

In order to create something bigger than ourselves, what we build and create must enrich lives in some way. How do you help others through your product, services, or project? Don't think that contributing and communing has to be charitable. In his book, *Start With Why*, Simon Sinek claims people don't buy what you do they buy why you do it. Why are you so passionate about your product, business, or service? Why bother with all of this work to build this thing of yours? How will it help people? How will it make lives easier? Even those who may start a business only to make money soon realize the impact they have on the lives of their clients, colleagues, and the marketplace. Not to mention the benefit your life's work could have on your family and friends. If the business is not enriching the lives of those it touches, it probably won't succeed. One could argue that everyone is going to make an impact, either positive or negative, so what will your impact be? What legacy will you leave behind? When things get tough, what is the *why* that will give you the strength to keep moving?

This motivational book is one of hundreds, if not thousands, of its kind. I realize I am not writing anything all that new or earth shattering here. But, I feel compelled to write. I have a conviction that there are people within my circle of influence that need to read what I feel called to say. Just as you need a tribe, Seth Godin tells us in his book, Tribes, there is a group out there that is waiting for you to lead them. **What if, because you choose fear over starting, choose wandering over climbing, someone somewhere misses out?** What if your idea is just what they need to hear, but they never hear it because you were too chicken? What if your product is exactly what they need but they never get to use it? Because you were afraid of heights? Because you would rather sit on the couch and watch *Game of Thrones* for hours instead of hunkering down and finishing that design? Granted, *Game of Thrones* may just be worth it. Pretend I said *Real Housewives of Somewhere*. There, now I've offended at least one reader. Moving on. Remember what we already covered — you have gifts as specific as your DNA. *Only you can offer them.* Now take a moment and realize someone out there may desperately *need* that gift — your gift — in their life. How selfish of you to sit on the couch night after night! It's okay. Tonight will be different.

The Common Threads

If you are still struggling with multiple passions, look for the common threads within your various passions and career changes. I know that I want to inspire and encourage others. Those are two elements, two common threads, which have been constant along my entire journey. I also have a gift for seeing others' talents that they may not see, and a knack for helping fill the holes in their plan to share those gifts. Having taken the time to figure these things out about myself gives me a filter — a "why" — for course corrections as I climb. I am never going to go back to sitting and designing at a computer all day.

The common threads should help you land on your "why," and your "why" is the filter that will keep you focused and guard you from entrepreneurial ADD. It will allow you to quickly say yes to projects that fit your gifts and easily say no to projects that don't. It is liberating to have that filter and be able to assess opportunities quickly and accurately. On pages ix and x, think through what kind of tribe your mission lends itself to. By thinking through who they are and how they tick, it will be easier to find them. Craft a mission statement for yourself that reflects how you will enrich the lives of your tribe members. We've discussed the "why" and some of the "what," up next we talk about the "how" of starting your business and leaving your job.

Part 2. FOCUS YOUR EFFORTS

38

4

Learn Before You Launch
Make the Most of Your Final Employed Days

> "If you have almost any white collar job, you don't have a job, you have an opportunity."
> *Seth Godin*

If you can quit your job to launch your solo career right now, congratulations! I hope this book helps with that process. It is more likely, however, that you have to do some serious work in the foothills. In this chapter, we'll discuss how to do just that, including three ways to get a promotion while you work towards being ready to go solo.

Congrats on Your New Gig!

Right now, it is imperative that you realize you have a new job and a new boss. I'm giving you a promotion right this second. "But Kelsey, you just said I'd have to do work in the foothills." And you will. For Yourself. **You now work for you, from now on, no matter where you're employed or what you're doing.** You are now working towards your end goal, no matter what. What does that mean?

First, it means that you start building your business now. You're going to start rethinking your dreams, goals, time, hobbies, income, expenses, even what you post on social media. There is almost no risk of starting your dream on the side while still employed. What can it hurt? What's the worst that can happen, you change your mind? You get distracted? Your product idea flops? How much better to do all of those course corrections *before* quitting your full time job!

Second, it means that you need to start treating your current job or position as training. Absorb as much as you can and add value wherever you can. I'll expand on how to do that in this chapter. Not only will the work in these chapters prepare you for breaking out on your own, they can also get you recognition and maybe even a promotion while you wait!

When I began at my final place of employment, I was hired as an entry-level designer, though I had years of experience. That was the position available at the time. In the first week on the job, I got bored quickly, since first weeks are filled with starter projects, personality tests, and paperwork. I took this downtime as an opportunity to audit my new workplace. I quickly found that the agency had no social media platform or plan. By the end of my second week, I had written a plan and scheduled a meeting with my brand new bosses to present said plan. It felt a little crazy at the time — they had hired me two seconds ago and here I was presenting about social media, 100 percent *not* a part of the job I was hired for. Included in my presentation were an executable plan and some goals. I was basically placed in a new position and given more responsibility on the spot. I added "social media guru" to my title on LinkedIn and gave the whole office a short how-to presentation about social media. Here is the lesson. If you can solve a problem that your leaders didn't know was there, you create a need for yourself and add value immediately. I did this same process again later to eventually become Associate Creative Director. I am not saying any of this to brag, I'm saying it to provide credibility for my next point:

You Don't Wander into a Promotion

In most cases, promotions do not just happen to people. A raise may happen every six months or a year, but not a promotion. All of the working, initiating, leading and self-promoting you do while still employed acts as strength training for your climbing muscles. Getting a promotion now can help you save more money towards quitting and provide more clout for when your Big Opportunity happens to see you on LinkedIn.

Not sure where to start? First, realize that everyone starts at the bottom. Even when you leave your job and venture up to your peak as a solopreneur, you're at the bottom of that new climb. A major pitfall I see with young aspiring solopreneurs is they want to do the work of veterans and be treated like veterans.

I most definitely had this problem straight out of college, as most recent grads do. You can only be an elitist after you've earned it. Are you in your 40s or 50s and still creating great work? Then congratulations, you've earned it. Not there yet? Don't worry, you will not be in the flatlands forever, and this book will hopefully help speed up the process, but remember you have to start somewhere. When you're just starting out, you are not too cool for the work or the client. Only wanderers are too cool. Understand that you *will* get to the point where you can be selective about the projects you do — that's the whole point of going solo — but it's going to take time and effort to get there. Just think of it as training and make the most out of each training day. We'll discuss this more in Chapter 6.

Your Leader, the Iceberg

I hope your leaders are not as cold as ice (Insert cymbal crash and laugh reel here). That is not what I'm talking about by iceberg, though if they are cold, I feel for you. It has been said that great leaders are like icebergs — you only see the tiny top portion of all that they do for you. Even not so great managers probably have more on their plate than they can handle. One way to position yourself for a promotion is to add value to those leading the way ahead of you.

Become the go-to, right hand helper of your leaders. They will appreciate the help and you will get to see under the surface of the water, learning about your leader and what it is really like to hold their title. See what you can learn from them that will help you run your own business or manage virtual team members or collaborations one day.

I believe one of the most under appreciated attributes is resourcefulness. Tony Robbins has said about successful people, "The defining factor is never resources, it's resourcefulness." There is not much more annoying to a leader than to have to hold someone's hand on a project, especially if the resources are out there. Before you go to your boss to ask questions, unless it's truly something only they can answer, try and find the answers for yourself. Just like the right hand helper adds value, so does the go-and-do-it-er who knocks things out of the park without constantly asking for guidance or reassurance. In your solo business, resourcefulness can make the difference during a month that is more famine than feast. Practice resourcefulness now while the pressure is low.

Another attribute that will set you apart in today's insta-economy is thoroughness. Many times eagerness about the project (or about getting the project over with!) causes us to rush a project's initial stages, which are the most important. Don't jump into creation too quickly. Ask 100 questions, pause, think and ask 100 more. It's tempting to dive in and tackle that scary white page, but great work is backed up with great research, which means you have to actually do said research. If you're writing some lines and getting some sketch ideas in the first project meeting, you may be on to something, but chances are it will only be one 100th of a percent there. Even on the tightest of deadlines, take a few minutes before you get started to really think through your overall goal and your initial tasks through before you start creating. When you launch out on your own, keeping your cool and backing up your work with great research will set you apart from competitors.

But, what if you are already adding value and killing your projects, but you are stuck with an inaccessible leader? What if you work in a small company with no room for advancement? Here are three strategies to get a raise, change your title, or even move to the next stop in your career path, even if there are no openings for a promotion at your current company.

1. Submit a Report

I know, that's not as sexy an answer as you were hoping for, but hear me out. First, you do not need to wait for your annual review. Did you catch that? *You do not need to wait for your next scheduled performance review!* Ask your boss for a meeting, in which you'd like to have a six-month review or yearly review, or whatever time line fits your situation. In your review meeting, you whip out your report, your personal Awesome File. If you work in the left-brained numbers-driven strategic part of the workforce, this should be fairly easy for you. You can easily show "Sales went up 10 percent due to the program I implemented." or "Here's a pie chart and a giant Excel sheet to back up the work I've been doing for the last six months! Yay, charts! Yay Excel!" On the creative side of things, it gets a bit harder but is still totally doable.

Your Awesome File is all of your finished work over those months, complete with the value you've been adding and the problems you've been solving. If you did an overhaul, redesign or rewrite, be sure and include the before and after. Collect every positive email about a completed project, from your boss, customer, or client, and include them as well. Make sure that you consider other achievements you have had outside of the work itself, like awards you may have received or if a website featured your work or a blog quoted you as an expert. Think to yourself, "How have I helped the reputation or image of the company with my accomplishments?" When you're kicking tail and taking names, that makes your boss, and the company, look good. Another question to ask yourself is, "How have I helped my team, improved morale, or improved internal communications?" Ideally, the answers to these questions will make your Awesome File practically scream "THIS PERSON DESERVES A RAISE!"

Now, when you have a sit down meeting like this, *you also need to be prepared to discuss any failed projects or less-than-ideal moments you had with your team or your leaders.* Think through all of the possible negatives beforehand and be hard on yourself. This way, when they come up you are able to address them. Explain how or what you have changed and why you are sure those things won't happen again. Be able to back up these claims. *If you're not ready to change, or need help on how to change, you're not ready for this meeting yet.* At the same time, if you put your file together today and it's less than awesome, it's time to up your game. It sounds like you've been wandering rather than climbing. That's okay, but that changes now. Take a couple months — yes, months — to add more content, help your team and add value to your leaders, and then set up this meeting. It sounds overwhelming right now but start by focusing on tomorrow. Starting a new project? Then make sure to gather the "before" data for your records. How can you add value tomorrow? Where can you help? Who can you help? Be more strategic, creative and intentional than ever before — you have an Awesome File to fill now!

2. Entertain Other Offers

Ahh, a much sexier option! You can definitely justify going in to your boss and straight-up asking for a raise or title change if someone else has offered you higher compensation. People who seem to skyrocket "up the ladder" are always interviewing, always growing, always networking, and always marketing themselves. Before I left my agency job to start my own business, I had been contacted by a headhunter, went to multiple interviews, and was approached by a various potential freelance clients, without actually leaving or telling my employer about it. However, I treated each opportunity like it could be the chance of a lifetime and sure enough, one of them eventually was. Think how easy it will be to prepare for — and rock at — interviews if you are keeping your Awesome File in order!

Obviously, the *huge* risk here — HUGE RISK HERE — is that your boss may say "Congratulations! I hope you love your new job!" and BAM you're out. So, always be interviewing and looking to see what's out there, but think long and hard before taking this approach with your current employer.

3. Ask for an Opportunity

This tactic would be best if paired with the aforementioned Awesome File, but you can always just ask *"What can I do to work towards a raise or promotion? Can we set a time line and a goal for me so I have something to work toward?"* You could go the extra mile and come up with a goal and time line and suggest it to your boss, thus making it easy for her to say "Sure! Great Idea!" If you do this, though, think of a goal that would benefit the *whole company,* not just you. Could you launch an internship program? Reorganize internal reports or archives? Finish a big internal project that's been on the back burner forever? Start a company blog or Pinterest account? Find a hole that you can fill.

If you're a stay at home mom, if you're stuck between jobs, or are in a situation where an Awesome File doesn't really apply to you, you're going to have to be even more intentional with your free time. Look ahead to where you want to go. If you want to go back in to your previous career after your kids are grown, for example, can you take a couple hours a week to volunteer in your field? If you're like me and can get sucked into reading article after article about the latest mom life hacks, maybe instead you could read the latest magazines and journals in your chosen field? If you want to change industries or totally change careers entirely, look for an internship or a local club you could join. Within your internship or your volunteer work, there you can look to add value and create a file of projects you took on just like it was a job. Also, remember that you are supposed to be enjoying the journey. If volunteering at the hospital or interning with a publisher sounds like torture to you, then going back to nursing or switching to publishing probably isn't the answer!

I didn't promise that working through your current landscape would be easy. None of these options are effortless. I know you're anxious to break free of the 9-to-5 shackles. But you know the saying, "success" only comes before "work" in the dictionary. The key here is to keep these options in mind, keep your Awesome File updated, and keep your eyes open for places to *add value.* If you do, these are processes that are intertwined with your day-to-day life, rather than an overwhelming task to perform every few months. I have included an Awesome File checklist to help you get started. It's also time to stop and reflect on the six ways you can add value where you are now, in order to prepare for your departure out of the foothills we call your "normal job." Start on page xi.

Next, since you'll be prepared and already working on your business, it's time to make it easier for your Big One — that large purchase order or first big retainer client, etc. — to find you!

5

Help Your Big Breakout Opportunity Find You

> "How dare you settle for less when the world has made it so easy for you to be remarkable?"
> *Seth Godin*

Everything discussed in Chapter 4 better prepares you for your Big One. The Big Opportunity that allows you to break out and start your climb to solo success sooner. Say that five times fast. Adding value in your current situation may be what lands you your dream first solo client. It may get you a hefty raise, allowing you to quit your second job and finish your book. It may simply mean you are more efficient and intentional at work so that you can leave earlier and work longer on your prototype in the evenings. In this chapter, we discuss simple tactics and tools you can use to make it easier for your Big One to find you.

Thanks, Internet!

Once you have your Awesome File in order and have started adding value where you are, it's time to use tools to make it easier for your Big One to find you. Thanks to today's technology, the Internet, social media, apps, and smartphones, dreams are more accessible than ever before. **Think of modern technology, when used effectively, as a big pulley system on the side of your mountain, quickly launching you upwards past years worth of climbing.**

My Big One was the moment a national brand approached me to handle all of their branding and marketing needs, and was willing to pay me more than my monthly salary to do so! With a signed contract in hand, I resigned from my dream design job and was able to start my dream, my own business. To an outsider, it may have looked like this *just happened*, but I assure you, it did not. I used the tactics outlined in this chapter to get where I am today and I am positive they will work for you to.

Personal Branding

I love the Rachel Quilty quote: "Look after yourself! You are your number one asset." Whoever you are, whatever you do, whether blue collar, white collar, strategic or creative, you need to own your own domain name. If you do not own yourname.com, you are wandering. If you do not have a site set up, you can at least redirect your URL to your personal Twitter profile or an online portfolio. If your name is taken, buy something similar, like .net or .tv. You could also set up a personal brand for yourself that is not your name. Be intentional with a non-name identity, however. It should communicate who you are, what you do, and most importantly, what you want to be doing. You want to attract the tribe of colleagues, clients and customers that wants to go on your climb with you, so be sure to make it clear where you're headed.

A blog could work well as a non-name identity platform, but again, be very intentional. Unless you are a personal lifestyle blog, you will later need to rename "Ramblings by the River" or "Oklahoma Original" because, though trendy blog names, they really communicate nothing other than location. Stop everything, go to godaddy.com or a similar registrar, and buy at least yourname.com. If you own it already, make sure it's renewed.

In addition to a website, it's time to have a professional personal email address. Yourname or your.name or f.m.lastname @gmail.com are all acceptable. An even better option would be to set up firstname@yourname.com using Google for business. At of the time of this writing that service is free up to ten email addresses. When The

Big One comes knocking on your inbox, nothing says you're serious like replying as "SmilesALot22@gmail.com"!

Having your own corner of the Internet is important for a few reasons. First, you own the content. Hopefully, you know by now that anything you post to a Facebook page or profile, or on LinkedIn or Twitter is owned by that social media platform, not you. Next, it establishes credibility immediately. Even though it may seem like everyone has their own website, so personal sites now have little value, I can tell you with total confidence that is false. Of everyone I know in the professional world, more *do not* have their own website than *do*, and I come from marketing! Lastly, a personal site is where you can really cultivate a brand for yourself and begin marketing yourself.

Even though I am dropping truth right now liked Diddy, in plain black and white for everyone, some of you still think this does not apply to you. Well, it does. If you want to move forward in your career — in any field — a website *will* help you. A teacher, for example, can catalog class statistics, praise from parents, deans, or principals, and share his personal teaching philosophy as it relates to what he wants to do next. An executive assistant can have before-and-afters, events they have planned, testimonials from a boss and references. Most importantly, both can have *a prominent objective statement explaining where they want to go next in their career.*

Are you thinking "Why not just use LinkedIn or Facebook for this information?" As discussed, you do not own the content posted on those sites. Beyond that, having everything in one place linked to all of your social media sites makes it easier for your ideal client or customer to find you. When interviewing for your next job, or networking, or marketing yourself — *which is 100 percent of the time* — you should have personal business cards on you. By personal, I mean not your company card from your employer. With personal business cards you can always send everyone you meet to the space that is 100 percent yours, designed and displayed in such a way that puts your climb in clear view and encourages people to join your tribe. It is much easier to remember yourname.com than behance.com/yourname or weirdblogname.wordpress.com. Plus, those long URLs can mess up the whole layout of your pretty business card design, am I right?

Your site can be a vital tool in taking you from the valley to the foothills of your dream. Once you've thought through the exercises in this book, make sure your site reflects *where you're headed,* not where you are. Many use their site or their social profiles as a resume, only showing where they've been. Here is an example of how to show where you want to go. James, the landman for an oil and gas company, has decided to start climbing and stop wandering, so he set up a website for himself. He has gone through this book and realized he truly wants to be a carpenter. He's been making custom furniture as a hobby for years. If you go to JamesLastname.com you will only read that he is a landman in one sentence buried deep in his about page. Now, he has a place to display all of his pieces. He has a blog where he writes about topics like "How To Restore Your Grandpa's Old Workbench" or "How Custom Carpentry Can Take Your Home From Ordinary To Extraordinary." He has gathered testimonials from custom furniture clients that are rotating on the homepage. He now has an online resume that shows not where he's been but where he wants to go. He keeps a simple business card on him at all times in case his "hobby" should come up in casual conversation. Could James gather enough carpentry work to quit his well-paying job without this online tool? Possibly, but like I said, the Internet is your personal pulley system, and when used effectively, can elevate you past years of climbing!

If you are a serial entrepreneur, try and be as concise as possible. With each revision of kelseyhumphreys.com, the music section, *which at one point was the entire focus of the site,* became less and less prominent. Your Big One — be it a publisher, that first big solo client, the customer who will place your first large purchase order, whatever — needs to be able to understand you from your site within seconds. Spell it out for them. Why do they want to work with you, buy your product, or invest in your Kickstarter?

If you're still working through multiple passions, it may be a good idea to have separate sites, and link to those sites back to yourname.com. Remember though to choose one — the one you've decided is your most promising next hill — to be clearly more important than the rest. Otherwise, viewers will be confused and leave having looked at none of it.

Market Yourself

Now that you have a little corner of the Internet that clearly shows who you are and where you're headed, it's time to start sharing. Before I was approached by my Big Opportunity, I posted occasionally on Facebook about what I was working on. I shared photos of finished work or my excitement to be speaking at a nearby university. I did not share everyday. I don't think I posted these kinds of posts even once a week. I posted enough for interested eyes to see what I was doing, but not enough to put off friends and family. That national brand found me because a close friend's younger sister worked in their corporate office. I used to think this somehow lessened my accomplishment of landing them as my first client, but I realized later that makes no sense. After all, I was the one promoting myself to my personal network and I had to go present myself to them just like any stranger would. This is a key point for you to remember: **your Big One is already connected to your personal network somehow.** Makes you want to rethink your rant about the president or the Oscars now, doesn't it? You don't want to over-share and annoy your friends and followers.

Once you have your goals figured out, it's time to start sharing information in an intentional way. Think of your body of posts on each platform as a pie chart. On Facebook, a primarily personal platform, the main portion of the pie from your profile (not a business page) would be personal, and a small sliver would be promoting your business. Once you start adding business associates as Facebook friends, you may want to create lists within your Facebook network so that not everyone sees all of your content. This is easy to do in Facebook's settings. On Twitter or Instagram your pie chart will look different than Facebook. No pie chart should have more than three or four post categories. For example, James the carpenter could have the following categories; personal, his work, carpentry teaching/tips, and interior design. The key is to think all of this through instead of spraying content of all topics and levels of intimacy across all platforms equally. Remember your objective and your filters as you come up with categories. If this seems impersonal or forced to you, I understand, but the clearer you are about your climb, the easier it will be for your tribe and your Big One to find you.

Fund-Raising Posts

I must note here that one surefire way to deter your Big One is if your connections think that your only goal is to sell a lot of { insert multi-level marketing product here } or to grow your downline of that product. If you are using some other product or side job to raise funds for your dream, I totally understand. If posts about those products are dominating your pie charts in every social platform, however, there is a good chance someone connected to your Big One will have hidden you from their newsfeed by the time you get around to sharing about your book launch, business offerings, email sign up, etc.

Start Your Conversation

It may start to seem, as you study your market, that everyone is doing tons of self-promotion on social media. Look through all of the tweets and feeds though, outside of your colleagues and competitors, and you'll see that the majority of people are still talking about what they just ate, sharing cat videos and gushing about what they're watching on TV. Stand out from the crowd by sharing your passion with others in strategic posts that matter to you and affect your climb!

Though social networking sites should not be your home base, you should definitely use them to market yourself. Set a reminder on your phone to check LinkedIn every other week. Set a separate reminder to update the online version of your Awesome File every other week and then post links to it on all of your networks. Take a few minutes each month to find new influencers to follow, blogs to subscribe to and new social media sites that might be worth joining.

This is another place where climbers set themselves apart. Wanderers cannot seem to find an hour or two per month for simple tasks like these. Climbers set smart phone calendar alerts, mark on physical calendars, put post it notes on the walls — whatever it takes to remember to invest in themselves and their journey!

But What About Blogs?

Everyone might indeed be starting blogs right this second; however, everyone is also abandoning those blogs. As of 2012, Blogging.org reported that 65 percent of bloggers hadn't touched their blogs in a year or more. The key is to keep blogging, even if the marketplace is full. The blogs that stand above the crowd are the ones that have been around a while and are updated regularly. If you enjoy writing and you are posting about your true passions, it should be easy to stick with it. Don't start a blog just for blogging's sake, especially if you do not like writing! This is a common peak people want from afar; thousands of followers, guest posting on popular blogs, selling ad space and products. But that's a climb that takes daily writing and a lot of technical time tweaking — or paying someone to tweak — the administrative backend of your Wordpress site.

I have created a checklist for you to get started with your personal branding and marketing. This is a vital step and a fun one! Enlist help with website, logo and stationery designs if you need it. Finally, you are investing energy in yourself and your climb! You're building up your climbing muscles already! **You are worth the investment!** See these exercises on page xiv. Next, let's start setting your pace. You are starting to realize what you want to do, how you want to do it, and why, now let's dive into when!

6

Set Your Pace for Success

> "Adopt the pace of nature: her secret is patience."
> *Ralph Waldo Emerson*

When you start studying master climbers, and when you find fellow climbers to do this thing called life with, it's hard not to compare paths. We all know "comparison is the thief of joy," but even harmless study can bog you down if you're not careful. When realizing I wanted to change my business to a consultancy and start speaking and coaching with this book launch, I was overwhelmed by the marketplace. So many talented authors and speakers! Everything has already been said and done. I was flooded with beginner questions: "How could I ever start without a book?" "Could I really turn all of my notes and blog posts into a book?" "How could I get speaking gigs when I've only spoken a few times?" "These bigwigs have full calendars and multiple books and five e-courses!" But, comparing myself to Tony Robbins is silly — he's been climbing for decades! Decades! Don't compare your foothills to someone else's peak.

I recently read an amazing concept from Donald Miller, the author of *Blue Like Jazz* and founder of the Storyline conferences. In his blog post "The Failure of Twenty-Something Thinking and Why You Should Peak at 65," he asked readers to think about when they wanted to reach their peak. Do you want to peak at 30? 35? Do you really want to reach your personal mountaintop so early in life? Of course not! Haven't you seen the basically all the movies — the disciplined nerd gets wildly successful many years later, while the jock who peaked early works at the local car-mart! Wouldn't you rather peak closer to 65?

We live in the age of now. Want to get directions to that restaurant? Google tells you right now. Want to eat a warm meal or drink a hot beverage? Microwave it in two minutes. Stream whatever you want online instantly. You can get almost anything shipped to arrive the very next day. It's no wonder we feel like success and accomplishment must also be achieved with the click of a few buttons. While you're looking at your dream and all you want to accomplish, are you trying to squeeze it into a year? A decade? Realize that the climb is a long one. It's a journey, a marathon. That may not sound as sexy as a sprint, but do you want to sprint to a 9-to-5 future? Wouldn't you rather climb the long haul to launching your invention? Wouldn't you rather build up your online business for the next two years so you have the freedom to travel the world sooner?

Thinking about reaching a destination at 65 is hard for my generation and I bet it is all but inconceivable to the upcoming generation. There is liberation in the fact that you do have time, however that much time can also feel like heavy weights keeping you down. "I have to wait until I'm 65?! That is an eternity from now!" Well, remember, that after Chapters 2 and 3, **you're narrowing down your path so that the whole journey is enjoyable.** Forty years ahead of doing this thing that you love and want to keep doing anyway! Forty years of getting better and better until eventually, you are the master of it!

When it comes to pace, no one can go at full speed from the time they start to the time they peak. You will take breaks between now and then. You'll reflect on where you've been, you'll assess what parts of the climb have been best so far, and maybe you'll change your course. Maybe you'll totally rearrange your business model or list of products or services. It was a period of rest and course correction that birthed this book. To stop wandering and start climbing you don't have to see the whole picture, you just have to set a course that leads to a life on purpose, not a life filled with regret.

Managing the Daily Climb

I have shared how having a newborn allows for a lot of thinking time, particularly in the wee hours of the morning. Well, a few months later, that newborn has turned into a little person, and suddenly I am learning the concept of time as an investment. When you only get two hours in the morning and maybe two in the afternoon, you will definitely make a plan for that precious time. You'll realize very quickly that dust bunnies in the corner and piles of clean laundry are completely unimportant. When family or friends come to visit, you can say "Excuse the mess, I'm writing a book!" or whatever your dream may be. It feels so good to look at the dust bunnies at the end of a long day and yell to them "I'm writing a book! So there!" Except I don't really yell because that would wake the tiny human. I'm sitting quietly with my laptop on my couch, surrounded by toys, covered in spit-up, hair unwashed, PJs still on, but daggumit I'm writing a book! Huzzah!

You may not have an infant, but you probably have a list of have-tos. You have to go to work in order to pay the bills. You have to make time for your friends and family. You have to do laundry at some point. You know what you don't have to do? You don't have to read that novel right now. You don't have to get on Facebook, or Tweet that hilarious 140-character thought.

Brian Tracy was the first to really help me "get" this time as an investment concept. In his e-book *Discovering Your Talents* he talks about how businesses go through strategic planning. A company will sit down in a focused meeting, or more likely multiple meetings, and establish what they are best at, what should be removed from their portfolio, and most importantly, what services or efforts yield the highest return on investment. Tracy asks the question what would happen if you approached your time in the same way? If you make it a habit, it will change your daily life, without the sit-down strategy session (though that couldn't hurt). Here is what I mean: You wake up in the morning and get ready, take a 20 min shower, dress, etc., grab coffee and head to work. In the car, you listen to your favorite morning show and arrive to work. You go through your morning, decide to work through lunch at your desk, then before you know it, the day is over and you head home. At home, you make dinner, sit to relax and watch maybe three hours of TV, and head to bed. There is nothing wrong with this day; please hear me say that. What I'm talking about is different for each person and may be different *each day*. Let's dissect the day:

You wake up in the morning after eight hours of sleep and get ready, take a 20 min shower. What if you took a 15 minute shower and actually made breakfast for yourself — which everyone in the educated world knows is the most important meal of the day? Your answer may be, "Well, there is a breakfast bar at work so I don't need to do that" (Um, where do you work, Google?). Next!

You dress, etc., grab coffee and head to work. In the car you listen to your favorite morning show and arrive to work. What if, in the car, you listened to a book you've wanted to read? Or if you prayed? Or if you listened to an album of "pump-you-up" tunes? Your answer might be "Well, I listen to NPR and get to work feeling educated and informed, so I don't need to make a change." That's cool, because what we're talking about is the return. If you want to feel inspired one day, having felt draggy and lame that whole week, then the return on that particular commute would be better if you listened to a pump-up mix of tunes rather than NPR. Make sense?

You go through your morning, decide to work through lunch at your desk, then before you know it the day is over and you head home. Working through lunch is admirable, but going to lunch with your boss, attending a networking event, or having lunch with an influencer in your field might have a much higher return than sitting and finishing that project. Some days the answer might be that you'd rather work through lunch to get home to your family earlier which has a much higher yield. I'm not saying either option is right, many options are totally fine.

    I watch too much TV. There, I said it. I know a lot of creative entrepreneurial types who are much better about this. They get home from work and read, write, or go to plays, all of which tend to have a higher return in terms of feeling inspired, relaxed, and connected to community. In a lot of cases, those activities even have a higher return in terms of entertainment value than the ol' boob tube. But there will be days that you really need to sit with your feet up and watch mindless TV for your mental health. Or, like me, you may choose sitting and writing over cleaning the house six days out of seven, yelling at those dust bunnies with the passion of a thousand suns, but on that 7th day cleaning the house may actually give you more satisfaction. Clutter has a way of hindering creativity after a while.

    Are you starting to get it? To live out what I'm talking about, you have to mentally pause throughout your day and assess your mental state, the state of your day, and figure out the return. What if instead of eight hours of sleep you woke up an hour earlier to meditate? To work out? To sit at your journal and write? What activities return the highest yield for you personally?

    There is a small risk here that when you start to analyze the return on invested time, you will ask "What will make me happiest in this time?" or "What can do the most for me?" But keep in mind doing the work towards your dream may not always be the most fun or happy option. Sometimes pouring out and giving does a lot more for us than taking in or consuming. Look for people and places in your day that need what you have to offer. If you have a free hour, could you call a team member who you know is discouraged? You are leading the way and people are following behind you, how can you give back to those followers and add value with a spare half hour here and there?

Maximizing Your Time

When evaluating your time like this, you should start to notice, if you don't know already, when you are most productive. If right before the lunch hour is your sweet spot, try and make that time climbing time. For example, ask your superiors for a solid chunk of interrupted time before lunch each day, no meetings, calls, IMs or emails then if possible. Then use that time on a big project that will fill your Awesome File. At home, if you are an early bird get up a bit earlier, or if a night owl stay up later, so that you can have some time away from your other obligations. Use those precious high-productivity hours for your dream, not checking Facebook or playing Candy Crush. Make that block a no-email, no-phone, no-nonsense chunk of climbing.

If we all did this each day we would be some truly amazing individuals, wouldn't we? We'd feel content, refreshed, inspired, connected, etc. We'd learn to say no to things that leave us feeling drained and say yes to people, events, and activities that leave us feeling better. We'd be strategically investing in our dreams daily, versus haphazardly on the weekends. **You can do this, it's not rocket science. It's not just for the "organized types" or executives with time set aside to plan their week.** Anyone can take time to plan their week or their day. One of my favorite Benjamin Franklin quotes reads: *"Do you value life? Then waste not time, for that is the stuff of which life is made."* The stuff of which life is made! Your time and talents need to go where you get the highest return! You deserve that return, and the world needs the best you that you have to offer.

Managing Your Thoughts

While you're taking stock of your time, you should also take stock of another precious commodity, your thoughts. Margret Thatcher said once: "What we think, we become." That is a powerful reminder to stop all the negative self-talk and doubt going on in our minds! Remember, successful climbers are positive, upbeat people. If you carry a Negative Nancy around with you in your own mind, she will slow you down like a bag of boulders. The apostle Paul wrote in the Bible that renewing your mind is transformative. What you reap in your mind you sow in your soul, so what are you sowing? Are your reading too many depressing books or watching too much disturbing television? Your thought life changes your actual life. Instead of focusing on how your feet hurt and your load is so heavy, look at how far you've gone already! Look up to the peak and remember the dreams that started you walking in the first place. Pray over your goals during your daily meditation time. Focus on your strengths and not your weaknesses. Do whatever it takes to get and keep your mind in a positive place.

    Master climbers — how do they stay so annoyingly positive? Various studies have been done on the power of optimism and positive thinking. In the massively successful book, *The Secret,* Rhonda Byrne claims that you get what you focus on, an idea called the Law of Attraction. Others talk about this idea as "manifestation." Whether you believe the idea or not, there's definitely no benefit to focusing on negative thoughts. Don't spend your passion on anger at your parents, your boss, your coworkers, "The Man." I know what you're thinking and no, we don't live in a bubble. Yes, crap happens. I am not advocating living like an emotionless robot or trying to appear "Facebook Perfect" at all times. We all have down days, especially if you have a five month old and you're trying to write your first book and figure out how to get an album removed from iTunes. But, focusing on the negative and feeling the negative are two different things. What I'm talking about is *habitual* thinking. If you have a habit of thinking only about your faults and how you suck and your job sucks and your life sucks — guess what? Everything will continue to suck. Again, not rocket science, but something so hard for us to remember. Along your path you will find plenty of haters, you don't need to carry one with you! Be vigilant about protecting your thoughts.

    I have included some dream planning and time management worksheets to help you set your pace on page xviii. There are many other books that go into great detail about making the most of your time, for starters I recommend the free resource from Donald Miller found at storylineblog.com, *Getting Things Done* by David Allen, *Make Today Count* by John C. Maxwell, and *Eat That Frog* by Brian Tracy. Next up we talk about smoothing the transition from dreaming to doing, from side-hustle to solo career!

Part 3. FULFILL YOUR PURPOSE

7

Prepare for Your Departure

"The first step toward success is taken when you refuse to be a captive of the environment in which you first find yourself."
Mark Caine

Walking towards your mountain means leaving the valley behind. To head towards the life you want, you will have to leave where you are. Let that sink in. This is another reason why so few reach their peak in life. Most of the time, success and fulfillment lie outside of our comfort zones. **It's called a climb, not a ride.** Your solopreneurial peak does not just suddenly appear under your feet. You will have to face the fear of leaving the little hut that you've made so cozy down in the foothills. Leaving is scary. Leaving takes effort. Yes, your little hut is familiar and easy to maintain now, but will it still be warm and cozy in 20 years? In 10? Or will it be cramped and musty, reeking of regret. Regret that you didn't apply for that better job. Regret that you never sat and wrote out your children's book idea. Regret that you didn't invest in your prototype when you had the time and energy.

Leaving the valley also means leaving the valley dwellers behind. Hard work and dedication are not always fun or popular. There will be blood, sweat and many tears. Staying in the valley is easier, 100 percent guaranteed. But, this is your life's work! This is your life's story! You can't expect, and truly don't want, for it to be a fluffy, sweatless walk in the valley. Some friends may never leave the valley. They may not want to climb with you or even volunteer to be your cheerleader. They may want you to stay in your hut because they are too scared to leave their hut. You've heard the one about pecking around with chickens when you're meant to soar like an eagle. Chickens are just that — chicken. Don't let *their* fears hold *you* down.

Along with Chickens comes an entire group of Negative Nancies. They will tell you it's not worth trying. They will tell you planning out your life is lame. They will say you have time to plan later, now it's time to just have fun! They will try and tear down anything you build up because they haven't built anything of their own. You are going to have to surround yourself with fellow climbers. Better yet, find a climber who has reached great heights and see what you can learn from them. Be warned, climbers tend to be positive, driven, go-getters. If you only want to be around cynics, those cats that are too cool for school, you may not be ready to leave the valley after all.

If You Married A Nancy

I have been asked, well what if my spouse doesn't support my dream? That is a tough question, with so many personal factors to consider. At the start, however, it is probably safe to assume that they are operating from a place of their own fears. Sit down and ask them what, specifically, worries them about your dream to go solo. You will probably have to do some proving to them that you are committed; that you have done your research, and that you're in it for the long haul. To be honest, you will probably have to do the proving for quite some time before they really get on board. Think of them as the investor that they are, just like you would work to convince a VC to invest, you need to show your spouse that you're serious. You will have to do the proving when the rest of the house is sleeping. No big deal though. You have taken the time to choose the climb that's right for you, so doing some initial prep for your journey in order to get him or her on board is no sweat. Think of it as extra training.

Climbers are always training, moving, and going. They're not talking about climbing, they *are* climbing. Almost everyone has dreams they talk about. Entrepreneurs always have a dream brewing. Creatives always have a project in the back of their head. A key difference between a valley dweller and a climber is valley dwellers are all talky and no walky. Yes, I just wrote that and no, I'm not deleting it.

The Spinach Trap

Climbers do not fall into what I like to call the Spinach Trap. In today's overly informed readily inspired online world, everyone knows they need to eat more spinach. Someone posts an article on Facebook about how to easily sneak more spinach into your diet. Jenny follows the link into a deep rabbit hole of spinach-in-eggs, spinach-in-smoothies, spinach-salads- that-don't-suck recipes and ideas. She feels educated and healthy just from reading all of the information and filing some away on her Pinterest board. She actually buys some spinach the next time she's at the store. She starts talking to others about the importance of spinach and shares all of her knowledge with them, feeling like a regular health guru. Everyone admires her efforts to get healthy. However, that night when she gets home a salad sounds lame and she orders pizza. She thinks "Eh, I'll put the spinach in a smoothie the next morning." The next morning she presses snooze five times and skips breakfast altogether. By the end of the week, the spinach has gone bad and she tosses it, but she still feels better about herself for at least buying it. Therein lies the trap. This false sense of accomplishment continues for weeks until she eventually forgets all about spinach. Her diet is 100 percent the same. With access to more information and inspiration than ever, the spinach trap is almost an epidemic, but The Spinach Epidemic sounded too dramatic. People are learning how to be healthier, how to be a better leader, how to use life hacks to save time, how to do a million things. They're learning but not applying. They have a million ideas for a business or a product or marketing campaign but they never launch. They're — you guessed it — wandering. Climbers absorb and then actually apply what they learn. They don't share information just to seem educated and impress others. Climbers actually eat the spinach.

Sharing Your Dream

So when *should* you start talking about your new goals and ideas? There are two different schools of thought about whether or not to share goals with others. Some say sharing your goals makes them real and attainable. It can also form a connection between you and others with similar goals. Most importantly sharing provides an audience that can then hold you accountable. If you haven't been one to dream aloud in the past and you've been shoving your dreams down into your gut — I say get it out, man! Once you achieve clarity and make a commitment, scream from the rooftops.

The other school of thought is that you are more likely to reach a goal you keep to yourself. In 2009, New York University published a research article, *When Intentions Go Public,* which confirmed my Spinach Trap theory is real. The study showed that by simply sharing their goals, half of the 165 participants felt closer to having achieved it. If you are like *someone* I know well who was going to be a pop star, then a creative director, then a Broadway star and then an agency owner, hold your cards to your chest. I had to pause and take months and evaluate myself and my goals and dreams. That is what I hope you do, in less time, using this book. Once you've figured it out, let it marinate a while. Talk to your spouse, maybe your best friend, but hold it dear until you're well on your way out of your current valley.

Fellow Climbers

One way to find balance between the Spinach Trap and over-sharing your goals with the world is to find a mentor. I will be honest, this is not easy for me. I want to find a female mentor and the motivational business speaker/coach world is still dominated by men. Though there are some amazing women doing what I want to do, none of them are accessible to me right now. I decided to get some coaching for a specific part of my business and that is working wonders so far. Some way, somehow, find someone to learn from beyond just reading blogs and watching videos. Hands-on coaching and mentoring makes a huge difference.

Equally important, is finding a like-minded accountability partner. Dr. Matthews' study at Dominican University showed that the odds of achieving your goal went up about 15 percent just by having a friend or colleague to hold you accountable. Remember they need to be like-minded. This is your dream, your business, your baby, right? So, find someone who meshes with your core values as well as your business goals. Online support groups or local associations in your industry are a good place to start!

Never Say These Two Words

When you do start talking about your mountaintop and the climb ahead of you, don't minimize what you're doing. If only I had a dollar for every time I have heard someone start a sentence with "I'm just." Like my friend who is "just a blogger" with thousands of readers. "I'm just working to become a freelancer…." "I'm just an Etsy shop owner…" "I'm just a dreamer…" No, you're not "just" anything. You were made in God's image, with specific dreams and gifts! You can achieve more than you ever thought possible. You are starting at the bottom but you know who else started at the bottom? Steve Jobs, Oprah, J.K. Rowling, and Colonel Sanders. Michael Jordan and Bono and Beyoncé. You're choosing to leave the valley, which takes serious guts. The world needs what you have to give, and don't you forget it! Complete the fellow climber worksheets starting on page xx and list the Negative Nancies in your life, as well as the master climbers you can learn from.

8

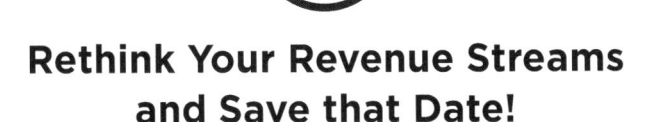

Rethink Your Revenue Streams and Save that Date!

'A dream is just a dream. A goal is a dream with a plan and a deadline.'
Harvey MacKay

After you have gotten into the rhythm of productivity and positivity we discussed in the last chapter, it's time for the fun to begin. It's time to plan your actual departure from the valley of the 9 to 5.

Research & Recon

Everything has already been done. It's true. But, as we already discussed, you're not going to let that stop you because you have your own voice and your own circle of influence. However, since everything has already been done, you might as well take some time to learn from other people's mistakes.

In your research that you conducted to choose the best climb for you, you probably saw some stand outs in your industry. What makes them a stand out? What can you learn from them? What holes have they left that you can fill? Who is doing your mission well, *both* locally and online? What topics do they cover in their content? How often do they update their blog/videos/content? What products and services do they sell? What is their business model? What kind of culture/lifestyle do they create/promote? How do they use social media? Who are they trying to reach? Can you focus in on a more specific group? Think about the questions and problems your target client or customer faces. What is missing in the solutions from your competitors?

The point of all of these questions is to answer one ultimate question: **How can you differentiate yourself from them?** Answer these questions on page xxii.

Beware! Recon missions can sometimes lead you to Shouldland. Do not try to copy a master. Do not try to take someone's tactics, change a few words, and call it your own. It's so easy to do! To avoid this, remember your mission. Your "why" is your own. After you spend time researching and coming up with some ideas for yourself, stop, drop, and roll away from your computer (or you can just walk away I suppose)! Clear your head and refocus on your mission and vision.

Get Down to Brass Tacks

By now you should be able to start calculating how long it will take you to be ready to quit your job. How big of a purchase order will you need, and how many hours will it take you to be ready for all of those orders? How many hours before you have your manuscript ready to pitch to traditional publishers? How long before you will feel ready to pitch to investors or venture capitalists? If you are a risk taker, and can stomach starting your journey without any signed contracts in hand, maybe you should consider how much savings you want to put away to provide yourself a cushion.

Now, I know it's not totally black and white. For many of us, freelance clients or consulting customers can't be estimated before you actually land the contract. However, you can start to figure out the pricing of your services, and how many clients or hours you'd need to fill in order to feel financially stable enough to break out.

Create Your Map

I am not going to ramble on about business plans. Some people need them, others don't. Personally, I landed a giant client right off the bat and had to simply stay afloat. There were written goals, some general ideas, but there was no formal business plan. If you are going to pitch to investors or ask for a loan, a business plan is a must. Either way, it is a good idea to have a plan beyond launching. If you get that giant purchase order or finally get three big-enough contracts, then what? Not only will a plan set you up for success and momentum, it will help you when you are scared out of your mind. Trust me, there will be moments when you are scared out of your mind. The more you plan now, before starting the climb, the easier it will be not to lose your lunch when you get to your first scary ledge!

Thanks Again, Internet!

Not only can modern technology can work as your personal pulley system as discussed in chapter 5 it can actually change the topography of your climb altogether. Topography is a big word. By it, I mean that the Internet, your smartphone and your digital camera may allow your goals to be achievable in ways you've never thought of before.

Let's continue using James the carpenter's story. It will take quite a few pieces of furniture a year to make up for his oil & gas salary, so James may need to change his perception of what it means to be a full-time carpenter in today's marketplace. Thanks to advances in e-commerce, he can now easily create and sell carpentry-related content as an added revenue stream. He could sell an e-book of how-to tips. He could host a monthly paid webinar that shows other would-be carpenters the dos and don'ts of custom carpentry. He could have a monthly subscription service that provides a newsletter to subscribers with how-tos, before and afters, and interviews with other master carpenters. Even though his target furniture client is not the group of carpenters, having a large following establishes credibility in his field.

I know what you're thinking — *"But if I teach others my craft, then won't I lose customers?"* You may lose a few, but most intend to learn a craft and never do, and those will end up buying from a seasoned veteran instead. You will have earned their trust by showing them exactly how you do what you do. This technique could work in so many applications; an illustrator who offers online illustration classes, a former teacher or daycare worker who sells monthly curriculum via a subscription fee, a designer or photographer who sells tutorials or templates. The list goes on!

Study successful climbers in all industries and see if there are any strategies you could apply in your industry. Think through what knowledge or services you could offer as online products. **How much better to add revenue in ways that are at least related to your dream, rather than just earning funds through a part-time gig you hate?**

Beyond selling informational products, James could target boutique furniture stores, his ideal furniture client, by creating an interesting documentary that shows the love, sweat and detail he pours into each piece. What used to take a lot of equipment and a production staff can now be achieved by just himself, his spouse or friend, a DSLR camera, iMovie and some appropriate background music. Easy peasy.

The landscape is changing all around us, with more opportunity than ever before, if you just take the time to strategically promote yourself. Please note I am talking about promoting *yourself*. It is unlikely you'll be able to hire an assistant if you're still working at your 9-to-5 job full-time, or if you've only just launched out on your own. I know a hugely talented author, professor, and consultant who could easily take his brand to the next level by moving some parts of his business online, but he's stuck with the "I need an assistant to do this for me" mentality. Or, if not his assistant, his daughter (Hi, Dad!).

There are many e-courses and webinars available online covering social media, website design, blogging, iPhone tips and tricks, DSLR cameras and much more. If you want a more traditional classroom experience, check your local community colleges and technical schools. Many offer continuing education or adult learning classes. These classes would be well worth the money and effort to put the power back into your own hands. No one is as passionate about your climb as you are!

When you start studying your niche, during your research and recon you may have found some online masters and now think *everyone* is becoming the next guru, all selling their online products. They are not. Remember many people still don't even have a website for themselves, never mind products and services that fit their passion! Think everyone is doing too much self-promotion online? They're not. You may just happen to follow a bunch of climbers who are all getting after it. You are learning from climbers and starting to use the web intentionally and that's a good thing! Once I started researching online marketing tactics for solopreneurs I suddenly found a million online marketers. Plus, they all use retargeting to follow me around wherever I go on the web (Google it and use it!). Same thing happens when you're in the market for a new car and you think you might want buy the new VW Bug, right? Suddenly your spouse's arm aches from all the slug bugging going on (Do people still do that?).

So, So, So Many Hats

You're not stupid. You know that staying employed is easier, with that steady paycheck, not to mention insurance and a 401k! Beyond benefits, you will also have to do, well, everything yourself. It may be worth planning a larger cushion or starting number so that you can hire a graphic designer for your identity and website design, someone to help you do taxes, maybe even a lawyer to help you set up your LLC. After going through all of the assessments in this book, it should be clear what you excel at and what you don't. Write out what you should outsource now, what you'd like to outsource soon, and what you'd like to outsource eventually. I immediately outsourced taxes and LLC set up. It was non-negotiable for me. Soon I would like to hire a virtual assistant to help me organize new products and programs. Eventually, I'd like to outsource all of the graphic design, which I currently still do myself. This solo gig can definitely get overwhelming at times. But! Remember, the majority of the work is work you love, and every single ounce of effort you put into your business directly makes an impact, you are not wasting that effort!

Save the Date

Make all of your calculations, estimates, perhaps guestimates, make them as conservative as you can stand, and then set a tentative launch date for your business. Start by using the worksheets on page xxv. With a date set, start treating your dream and "side hustle" for what it is — your main job, your real job. The one from 9-to-5 is just "fund raising" now. Your dream is for real now. It's serious. It deserves your time, effort, energy, excitement, and diligence. Next, since you're getting so close to launching, it's time take your personal brand and morph it into a business brand. You know what is gettin' real!

9

Branding Your Business for Success

> "A personal brand is your promise to the
> marketplace and the world."
> *Tom Peters*

I hope this is obvious to you, but it needs to be said. As a solopreneur, you are your brand. All of the tools from chapter 5 can be integrated into your business. If you want your personal self and your business self to be completely separate, going solo is probably not for you. Heck, working in the 21st century may not be for you!

What's in a Name

So, one of the first questions as you set up your business is the name. Should you be Your Name Consulting, LLC? Or how about Last Name Design? Events by Firstname? Well, that depends on your why/how/now and later. Remember, perception is reality. I decided not to use my name for my consulting business because I was going to be listed as an Agency of Record for a national franchise. Humphreys Design or Humphreys Marketing just didn't sound right for the services I was providing. At that time, I wanted to attract other larger food and beverage clients. Think about your dream clients or customers. What would they be drawn to? Are the services you create very personal? Do you do organizational consulting for giant brands? If you're in technology or programming, will your customers be expecting something made up, like "Google" or "Ubuntu"? Once you get into the mind of your customer, the decision should get a lot easier.

Another question to ask yourself is what your business will look like in ten years? Since you want to be a solopreneur, I am guessing you don't envision having 50 employees and a giant office building. If you do, however, and you put your name on the front door, almost all of these going-solo-guidelines still apply. If you're a consultant or contractor who hopes to have a few full-time assistants in the coming years, you may decide to go with something other than your name. **Either way, in almost every single small business instance, you are still your brand. People are choosing *you* when they choose your business.**

Your Mission is Your Climb

Before leaving my job, I had created a personal mission for myself that reads "Lift up every person and project that comes my way." From that, I created a theme for my business and even a name, Lever: we lift brands to the next level. My email signature is "Lift Up!" When I changed my business model and started writing this book, I rewrote my mission and a few words kept coming up over and over. Look at your Mission and Objective Statements you created. You should have a few paragraphs about your mission for others, along with who you want to reach and why. Now it's time to take those and repurpose them for your business. Pull out some keywords or ideas that you repeat or that are most important. Here are some examples: For the carpenter, James, his could read: Lastname Carpentry: Creating (verb) hand-crafted custom furniture and carpentry (noun) for the sophisticated consumer (who) looking for higher quality (why — implies options out there are low quality) accents in their home or office.

For a realtor, your mission may be "Helping (verb) home buyers find (verb) the perfect home for their family (who — families) to live their best life (why — passion beyond just houses)."

A personal trainer's could read "Guiding (verb) women (who) through the world of nutrition and fitness to make fitness and health easier than ever (why — ease)."

A freelance copywriter may use "Creating (verb) clear, compelling copy for publications and organizations (who) that produces real results" (The why here is passion for both clarity and results in their writing — implying no fluff).

How about a non-traditional example? An actress could use "Making characters come to life (verb) on the stage (who — meaning she is not trying to appeal to TV/Movie directors at this time) to tell stories the world needs to hear (why — passion for meaningful stories)."

My mission is now "to inspire and motivate (verb) solopreneurs (who) find their passion and focus their efforts so they can reach fulfilling their unique purpose in life (what)!" I still use Lever as the consulting arm of my business, and I still the lift up terminology throughout my materials because it works with inspiring and motivating others.

More than Words

Once you've got your mission for your business finalized, consider taking that statement and creating a slogan. Not all solo brands need this; sometimes the mission statement itself is enough. However for your website header or business card, a designer can usually do a lot more aesthetically with less words. With a concise slogan loud and proud on all of your materials, meticulously created using all of these exercises, **you are going to deter and attract the *right* potential customers.** I will continue with the above examples to get your idea juices flowing.

Lastname Carpentry: Sophisticated hand-crafted Carpentry. Low-budget shoppers, thrifters, and big-box shoppers will probably get the "too rich for my blood" vibe. He'll attract boutique furniture stores, high-income homebuilders, etc. Branding is a powerful thing! Next!

Lastname Realty: Love your home, love your life. This one is very broad, but in the next chapter we'll discuss how to use personal lifestyle and culture to attract clients when your slogan doesn't quite do the job on its own.

EZ Fitness by Firstname — Nutrition and fitness guidance for women. In this example, the name itself shows the why, ease, and the slogan is just a descriptor.

Firstname Lastname "Clearly Compelling" or even "Copy that Converts" would work as a no-fluff since her mission and why is to be direct and produce results. If he or she used a lot of fluff in her slogan it wouldn't work. **Your slogan cannot just be catchy, it needs to actually represent your mission.**

For the actress, Firstname Lastname: Great Characters Need to be Told — A play on great stories need to be told. Think how different this slogan would need to be if the actor is a comedian. In fact, if this person was a comedy player they should probably change their mission to include joy or encouragement or laughter.

Hopefully, these examples are sparking you to bridge the gap between your brand as you know it, and the five-ten seconds you get to make an impression. Coming up with a slogan is something that you will probably want to have someone else help you with. Even though we can get down to our mission and vision pretty easily, it is often a struggle to shrink them down into three-five words. I've included some worksheets to help you get started, but I strongly suggest giving these worksheets to a marketer or writer who can polish them up and edit them down.

More than a Logo

I am a trained designer (remember my second ear piercing!) and it took me until page 117 to get to talking about the logo for your business. And there are fewer things I love in business more than great logos! I really hope you get why. There is so much work to be done before you — or your hired designer — ever get to that blank piece of actual or digital paper. Having thought through everything on the last 116 pages is going to make your identity — your logo and set of branding elements — come together quickly and easily.

By now, you've spent a lot of time thinking about your ideal customer. You've got a name, mission and the beginning stages of a slogan, all catered just for them. Now, think about what you think would appeal to them visually. I can hear you "Kelsey, how the heck am I supposed to know that?!" Calm down, George. It's simpler than you think. For example, James, has decided to go after sophisticated, high-income buyers with his furniture, right? An obvious choice would be earth tones because he's a carpenter. There is something to be said for contrast, however, like using hot pink as his main brand color. A good reason to do that? Because he's decided to focus primarily on women, and the women in his target demo in his region (read: big city) will be drawn to it. Another good reason would be if he has chosen to design modern, funky pieces. That also lends itself to a bright color. If he is creating big traditional wood pieces, earth tones are the more logical choice, and could be paired with a primary color or maybe metallics, whatever his market calls for. **This is another place that a designer will do a better job than you will,** but I wanted to at least give you some insights.

Websites

Do not get rid of yourname.com. I repeat, do not get rid of yourname.com! If you only want to keep up with one site, then have that URL redirect to your business site. However, I want to explain why I think it might be better to use both and cross promote them. Remember, the world is your oyster in terms of online revenue streams. Within your mission, let's say you're a realtor and you landed on the mission earlier in this chapter, how can you go beyond realty? What if you decide you want to start speaking about realty and coaching other realtors that are just getting started? Additional revenue streams may not exactly fit on your realtor site. Some of them may, some of them may not, but all of them can work from yourname.com. Plus always remember the Google. They will look you up for any of your services and products by **your name!**

The What and The How

Hopefully, you're starting to see that there are many ways to fulfill your mission. How do you want to do it? What are the tasks that you want to fill your days? In ten years, are you still doing the same tasks or has your business changed? If you're launching a photography business, you may want to only do newborns and new moms. Maybe you have a passion for capturing those first few weeks of life, or even birth itself in the hospital. However the chances are, at first, you'll just have to book shoots. If you can't stand brides and weddings, take those off of the table, but consider building a "family photography" type of brand at the start. Another example would be the web developer who really wants to make his own software from scratch as his main source of income. At first, he may not land enough clients who are willing to pay for custom software, so to supplement he'll have to become an expert at fixing bugs in existing software, or perhaps rebuilding parts of various software platforms. I want to be a speaker/coach/consultant who writes. Not an author who happens to speak and coach. Right now, I am spending a lot of my time writing, but I am positioning myself for the *end* goal. You can position yourself for the end goal as well, but financially it will probably take some supplementation in the mean time to get there. For me, book sales are an important part of my current business model.

Start to transition your personal mission and brand over to your business on the worksheet on page xxviii with your *end* goal in mind. Luckily, after reading Chapter 8, you know that supplementing with additional revenue streams — streams that are associated with your dreams and goals — is easier than ever before!

Marketing Yourself as a Business

Content

Content marketing is basically giving away value to your target client in order to start a relationship with them and earn their trust. Trust eventually leads to loyalty and sales. This tactic used to be done via television and radio through traditional advertising, but now again, the Internet has changed the game and made it easier for small businesses.

We've already created content categories for social media posts, which now you want to basically expand on, since social media is a flash in the pan. Creating beefier content keeps them engaged with your brand longer. First think about what your ideal client or customer wants to consume — do they read blogs? Devour infographics? Watch a lot of online video? Maybe they listen to podcasts? Remember you don't need to be on every single social media platform, so you don't need to produce every single thing I just listed. Pick one or two that your tribe will love. Also, make sure you're picking something you can produce well, and produce regularly. Consistency is key in content marketing or else your tribe will lose interest and find someone else to get valuable information from.

I like the acronym by Mark Schaefer, which says to make sure your content is RITE — Relevant, Interesting, Timely and Entertaining. Also, make sure your content has a goal for your business beyond just adding value for your clients. Is the goal to start a conversation? Maybe your posts lead to an eventual sale, providing three posts with tons of valuable (free) content and then in every the fourth post or video or email you promote a related product. Other goals could be to increase your subscriber list or social media following.

When you post content, you'll want to promote it on your social media platforms. Another great way to promote content is through an email list that customers can subscribe to on your website. Email marketing and content marketing can be overwhelming but using the categories you've already set up for yourself, try and think of them as simply an extension.

Culture

If content is king, the queen is culture which means as a solopreneur in today's socially-driven culture, you have some serious advantages. Why is that? It's because consumers want to connect to people and values, not businesses and services. In many ways, social media has taken business back to the old days when small business owners traded with other small business owners that they knew and trusted. Since you are your business, you can use your personal brand to strategically appeal to your target like never before. Giving potential clients a glimpse into your lifestyle, values, processes and practices will set you apart from your competitors and attract like-minded people. Here are four ways to show your lifestyle in order to attract ideal clients, with some real-world examples:

1. Post Personal Photos. People want to connect with you before deciding to purchase your product or service. Small business owners should post more selfies. Yes, you read that correctly! Think about people you follow online and which posts of theirs are your favorites — the ones where you get to see a snippet of their life! It's like peeking behind the curtain, isn't it? Aside from images at the gym doing coaching sessions, personal trainers should also post styled images of meals, cooking in the kitchen, favorite fitness products in use, family time, dressed up for date night, church service, travel, etc. An author who writes about writing and creativity could use shots of himself at his laptop or in a coffee shop. He could also show photos of dinner parties with friends, the art gallery opening he attended, the downtown loft apartment he has his eye on, or even a series called "the state of my desk." Take note of how different this list would be if it were for an author who writes about working her way to becoming the CEO of a Fortune 500 company.

2. Post Relevant Quotes and Inspirational Images. Although they can get annoying in our feeds on our cranky days, as a Catholic friend of mine puts it, "Protestants love their quotes." The phenomenon goes well beyond Protestants; just open the Pinterest app. A professional organizer could post quotes about order, time management, peace of mind. If she is a woman of faith, she could also post verses about self-control, peace, discipline, etc. — anything relevant to getting and staying organized. If you create products for babies and children, you could post quotes and images about the wonder of childhood, how precious the first few years are, etc. You could also reach out to mothers (the ones purchasing!) and post things that would inspire them about motherhood.

3. Post Relevant Resources. You want to be seen as a go-to resource for everything related to your field. This means how-tos and tips from you **and** from other sources as well. Think outside of just posting about the work itself! An Interior Designer could post DIY how-tos on Pinterest, share related posts from women's ministries, share links to other blog's "before and afters" that she finds inspiring, not just her own finished projects. A realtor could post links about the changing housing market, how to stage one's home, best paint colors to choose when building a house, etc.

4. Show Your Work in Context. Instead of simply showing your finished project, show it in use in a way that will appeal to your target customer. Instead of simply posting a family photoshoot, a photographer could show family prints hanging on a wall of a warm, comfortable living room. If he books mostly friends from church that are middleclass, posting a shot of a gallery wall in a mansion would not make sense and would deter his core audience. A portrait artist could snap a photo of a portrait in progress on her desk surrounded by paint brushes and with the photo she's copying laying there as well, perhaps with a cup of coffee showing in the corner — all of that is so much more interesting than just a close up of the painting!

When you implement these tactics you'll notice more interaction from your clients — which means friends and colleagues of your clients are more likely to find you! You may deter a few people who don't share your values — but you don't really want them as customers anyway!

Putting it All Together

I want to hit my point home and the best way I can think to do that is with more examples. Hopefully, you enjoy examples or by now you're probably considering chunking this book in the trash.

    John is a people person who has decided to become a realtor. He goes through all the exercises and chooses to position himself for men who want to live the urban dream in the heart of the city. So of course, to start, he joins a company like Re/max and gets a page on that site. Next, John buys Johnlastname.com and on the site, he makes sure to have the Re/max logo and all of his Re/max credentials. At the top of the site, however he has his slogan "Live the High Rise Life." His site features images of amazing urban spaces. Also linked from his home page are resources to live the high rise life; recommended limo services, the florists with the best "morning after bouquet," where to find the "slickest power suits," you get the idea. He creates content in the form of a weekly blog post about city life and a monthly podcast where he showcases some of his favorite vendors. He posts Instagram pics from rooftop parties, jaw dropping properties, and his VIP access to the hottest clubs. On his Facebook page, he promotes his blog reviews of places in the city, and posts links to hot restaurants, bars, shops, concerts, *all near complexes where he has listings, of course.* He is strategic about it. Are all of his clients living the high rise life? Probably not yet. At the start, he might be selling his great aunt's house and helping his brother relocate to the suburbs. But, things won't stay that way for long. John is going way beyond just being a realtor. He is positioning himself as a city expert, appealing to a very specific person, thus making it easier for that person to find him.

Another, less black-satin-sheet-y example, would be a blogger who has been blogging on the side for years and wants to really make a go of it as a source of income so she can quit her boring job. She has just been a lifestyle blogger, but she went through the exercises and realized she really wants to empower women to feel beautiful and save money at the same time. She looks through her analytics and finds that her posts about shopping get the most hits. She also has quite a few followers on her Pinterest style boards. She decided to buy hername.com for her blog and put the slogan "Shop It Like It's Hot (and on Sale!)" at the top — quirky and fun, which she is. She linked to her blog prominently towards the top of her site. She signed up as an affiliate on Amazon and has a "products" page on her site that she recommends, and each product has its own blog post. The products could be anything from lipstick to the best bra to wrinkle spray for tough linen shirts, and she adds new products regularly after she tries them. She made a blogging schedule to ramp up Google traffic, and she makes sure that she promotes every post on Twitter and Pinterest. On Pinterest, she makes many more boards, each for specific styles, seasons, garments, and a few more on how to save when shopping, how to put together an outfit, etc. She reached out to locally owned stores to be a sponsor on her site, even though she didn't have much actual site traffic yet, a few of them said yes! She opened an Instagram account and posts chic outfits, close-ups of her make-up, pics of her out to dinner with girlfriends, walks with her dog, and snapshots of her styling one of her friends. She uses hashtags on those posts like there's no tomorrow. She reached out to local photographers to be a stylist for their shoots for free a few times to build a "stylist" portfolio. She only chooses shoots that would appeal to her readers and followers. She then added styling for photos as a service of her business on her website. She created a short e-book about saving while still looking chic that she charges five dollars for. She started pitching herself to blog conferences to do a workshop on "how to create your own style for your blogging image without going broke." There are so many more examples I could list but I feel like you get the point now.

To recap: Show lifestyle, personality and culture, all curated for who you *want* to attract as a customer. Write out all of your marketing ideas on page xxx.

Still not sure you have what it takes? Think it's too late for you? Have some other lame excuse not to start today? In the next chapter, I'll convince you!

10

Yes, You Can Start Right Now

> "The greatest amount of wasted time is the time
> not getting started."
> *Dawson Trotman*

Perhaps in the previous chapters you didn't come to an end business model or set business plan. It's too high up in the clouds for you to see it clearly. That's okay for now. You've gotten some great ideas about the kind of life you want to be living years from now, and you have something to walk towards. You've created a couple filters so that you can weed out the paths that are going to lead you to frustration and disappointment. Hopefully you can see that "Become a New York Times Best Selling Author" can be the same as "Get paid for sharing my message with others and being able to write for a living." Writing then could take on many different forms; it doesn't have to necessarily be a book or novel. That's the key. You're no longer wandering aimlessly. As you climb, things will become clearer. You will have to do less snazzy worksheets analyzing yourself and your passions. As you get closer towards your peak, you may see that you're not ready for the really tough parts ahead and you need to correct your course. You may get closer and see that what you once thought serene now looks like the gates of Mordor. You might realize that your peak is closer than you thought and gain momentum. But, you won't know until you **start now and stay diligent,** no matter how many course corrections you face.

    I know, without a doubt, my path seems ridiculous to some. I can't blame them, after all I went from a design career to a pop music career and back again. During that time, I had multiple blogs that I stopped and started. I thought about being a mommy blogger and selling designs on Etsy for about five seconds. I had a video series at one point and I plan to start one again. I ran a marina on a lake with my husband, but that's another story for another book (It may sound like a big vacation, but I assure you, it was not. Vacations do not include pumping poo out of houseboats and working outside 14 hours a day. But I digress). I literally don't know how many times I have redesigned kelseyhumphreys.com. Most recently, I am shifting gears again with the launch of this book. As I write it all out, I am feeling a bit sorry for my wonderful, ever-supportive husband. Like my parents and my "fall back" art degree, I'm sure he has had many moments where he was convinced I had lost my mind.

If you are an idea machine, a serial entrepreneur, I totally understand your hesitation to launch your next idea. Here are five reasons to pick yourself up and start again:

1. You learned from your last big idea. Maybe it failed, maybe it succeeded, either way you learned a lot. Just like you get better each time you cook a recipe, the same goes for initiatives and ideas. Ideas tend to birth other ideas. Maya Angelou said "You can't use up creativity. The more you use, the more you have." Critique yourself, brutally. Think through what you need to do better this time, and go for it!

2. Your core tribe members will follow YOU. Maybe you're concerned people will think "oh John, he's always doing something. Every few minutes he asks me to like a new Facebook page and follow a new thingamabob on Twitter!" And they may. Chances are they will like and follow long enough to see what this next one is all about. Why? Your tribe is following you, not your current, or previous, initiative. We have entered the Social Age and people want to connect with people. Brands are promoting their core values in a personal way. Business is personal. Social media is personal. Everything is personal. If you're connecting with people, they will keep following you. A bonus is you will find new followers with this new venture and your tribe grows. Will you lose a few? Probably, but then they weren't really part of your tribe anyway. There are many, many, many tales of big thinkers who failed at multiple things before hitting the Big One. Seth Godin said "If I fail more than you do, I win" Is this your Big One? It could be! The worst thing you can do is not try. Plus, to be "always doing something" is better than to be doing nothing! Good for you!

3. Your critics are watching anyway. Say it with me "Haters gonna hate!" No really, stop and say that aloud. Say it with attitude; maybe add some hand gestures. It feels good to say and it's true. Small people who are always there with an eye roll and a snide comment will probably never change. If you fail, they will not like you. Guess what, if you succeed they will still be there, not liking you. Remember you have a responsibility to the world to give and to do. You're out there doing things and they're sitting there watching you do things. Keep doing!

4. You have the guts to do big ideas. Creativity takes guts. Starting something takes guts. Putting out a blog, posting a design snippet to dribble, telling someone about your dreams, heck even posting a short video clip to Instagram takes some guts. We live in a share-everything world, with added pressure for the things we share to be creative, fresh, inspiring or at least interesting. Well, every time you've shared you've been thickening your skin. Do you need to say, "Haters gonna hate!" aloud again? No guts, no glory, and you've got the guts. Keep going for the glory!

5. You know what you want to do and will probably do it at some point anyway so why not get off your procrastinating, excuse-making butt and do it now?

Something is nagging at the back of your brain this very minute. It was probably nagging at you when you decided to download this book. That illustration series. That new blog. That video series you want to create. If there's not something nagging you right now there will be soon. That's how we're wired. King Solomon wrote, "Without vision, people perish." Fear wants you to stuff your nagging dream down and ignore it. Well it may be two years later or thirty years later, but sometime later you will not be able to ignore it anymore. How many years will you have wasted?

No, Really, Start Now

I love what Jon Acuff said about procrastinating in his book, *Start*; "Regretting that you didn't start earlier is a great distraction from moving on your dream today, and the reality is that today is earlier than tomorrow." Quit distracting yourself! If you feel like you've waiting too long and your ship has sailed, you're wrong.

If you are reading this book at 18, well, you're amazing and you'll probably be a United States President some day. Go out and make some mistakes, I wish you well. If you are reading this at 23, I hope this helps you to pause and evaluate so you don't make quite as many course corrections as I have made. Course corrections are not fun, and you will have some, to be sure. Going through these exercises should at least save you a couple.

If you are reading this book at 35, good for you. Like me, you have probably had just enough course corrections to realize it's time to get your you-know-what together. If you are 45 or even 55 and beyond, don't be discouraged. You have not peaked yet, and yes, you have time left. It may feel hopeless some days but it isn't. Many master climbers started their climb later in life. Don't believe me? Here are some examples!

Vera Wang started out as a figure skater who failed to make it to U.S. Olympic figure-skating team. She changed course and became an editor at *Vogue*, but was passed over for the editor-in-chief position. Changing courses again, she took it in her own hands and started designing wedding gowns at 40.

Julia Child took her first cooking class at 36. By the time she was 50, she published *Mastering the Art of French Cooking*. "To think it has taken me 40 years to find my true passion," she once wrote to her sister-in-law.

Winston Churchill, the Nobel Prize-winning, twice-elected Prime Minister of the United Kingdom struggled in school, even failing the sixth grade. After facing years of political failures, having been defeated in every previous election for public office, he finally became the Prime Minister at the ripe old age of 62.

Laura Ingalls Wilder, author of the best-selling series of books began with *Little House in the Big Woods,* (adapted one into the TV series *Little House on the Prairie*), didn't publish her first book until she was 64.

Peter Mark Roget was a man who envisioned a book that would not define words, but group them according to a classification, such as "space" or "moral powers." The first edition of *Roget's Thesaurus* was not published until he was 73, and he oversaw every update until he died at age 90.

Ray Kroc is the man responsible for the franchising of McDonald's, suggesting to the McDonald brothers that they franchise their operation across the nation. At the age of 52, despite battles with diabetes and arthritis, Kroc set out to build the McDonald's brand. At 59, he convinced the brothers to sell and became the owner of a franchise that would sell more than a billion hamburgers by 1963.

Colonel Sanders didn't become the fried chicken mogul we know and love until the age of 65! He then began touring the country selling Kentucky Fried Chicken franchises, and by the time he sold the business for $2 million in 1964, there were over 900 of them.

Takichiro Mori went from teaching to real estate at 55 years old, and went on to become Forbes' two-time reigning world's richest man with a net worth of around $13 billion in 1993.

Tim and Nina Zagat are the founders of the popular dining surveys of the same name. They were corporate lawyers until leaving their jobs to manage the business in 1986. Tim was 51 years old. In 2011, Google bought Zagat for $151 million.

Grandma Moses, or Anna Mary Robertson Moses, is one of the biggest names in American folk art. She was originally a big fan of embroidery, but once her arthritis grew too painful for her to hold a needle, she decided to give painting a try at 76. She lived another 25 years —long enough to see her $3 canvases go for over $10,000!

Joy Behar, comedienne and former co-host of *The View,* was a high school English teacher until starting her stand up career at the age of 40.

Andrea Bocelli started as a lawyer, moonlighting in a piano bar for fun and to make extra cash. He didn't catch a break as a singer until 1992, at age 34.

Harrison Ford started out as a carpenter. His big break was *American Graffiti,* but he got paid very little for his role. He decided he was never going to make it as an actor, and quit acting to get back into the more lucrative construction industry. He was cast as Han Solo by George Lucas (who directed *Graffiti*) when he was 34.

Ken Jeong, *The Hangover's* hilarious Mr. Chow, started as a doctor.

After earning his MD from the University of North Carolina, he began a physician practice and did stand-up jobs on the side. Jeong made his first feature film debut in 2007 at 38.

Ray Romano, aka Raymond in *Everybody Loves Raymond,* was a bank teller until a stand-up comedy competition launched his acting career in 1989, at age 32.

Start Where You Are

Everything I've read about writing a book says to write in the wee hours of morning, in a special place that is specifically for writing. Set the mood with a comfortable setting, the perfect cup of coffee, and let the inspiration flow. Some big-time authors have even rented cabins in the woods for weekends or whole months at a time! Ha! That was not my writing reality. Instead, at random times of day, I would put my infant daughter down for a nap, run to my laptop, and type feverishly until she woke up. I've already told you I'm on a toy-littered couch in my pajamas. I don't follow my own advice about waking up early or staying up late because my child doesn't sleep through the night yet. Lucky me. She does take pretty good naps, though, and so I am paving my own way. Maybe I'm a whole new breed of writer, the Working Mom Author. How glamorous.

Start With What You Have

Just like we stuff down our God-given dreams, we also tend to undervalue our own ideas. You already have some great ideas for your business, book, service, or project. Those ideas are probably what prompted you to pick up this book in the first place. Maybe they don't seem like much. This book is built from disjointed notes in my iPhone Notes app and unfinished notes on physical pads of paper everywhere. Why do I have so many different journals and notepads, anyway? It's ridiculous. I also kept a long, unorganized Google Document about entrepreneurship, leadership, creativity, and marketing. The term *document* is generous. More like *Google Word Swamp*. Or *Google Random Paragraph Mash-Up*. I started blogging every so often about quitting my job to start my business. If I had been smart, I would have also recorded audio bites on my drive to work, when I would often think up great ideas. With the new waterproof phones coming out, we can all start to take over the world, one idea-filled shower at a time!

Even if you can't do any of the *genius* ideas I've lined out for you in this book, you can still start right now, where you are, in some way. You can figure out a few next steps and start knocking them out like a boss, no matter what they are or what that actually looks like. Just strap on your boots and get climbing already! Take a few minutes to look back at your notes from Chapter 6, then, on page xxxii, write out some action items you can tackle right away. Remember the famous quote from Les Brown, "You don't have to be great to get started, but you have to get started to become great." Now that you're convinced and committed to your solo journey, in the next chapter I will give a few practical ways to stay inspired and diligent on your climb.

How to Stay Hungry
(After You're Bringing in the Bacon)

> After climbing a great hill, one only finds that there
> are many more hills to climb.
> *Nelson Mandela*

You are killing it with your business, making plenty of money from multiple revenue streams, feeling fulfilled, and getting to design your life. You're looking at the view from great heights and it's a beautiful one. But, if you're not careful, all that gazing at the clouds will cause you to miss a giant crevice along the way called complacency. Don't worry, this chapter will help you avoid it.

Not Really Solo After All

Very few make it to great heights all on their own. As you climb higher and higher, most of your tribe will stay on a plateau and watch. They will still be cheering you on, and they will be studying to see how you climb so they can follow your lead when they're ready. But, they are not going to face the wind and the cold with you. Few will. At the top, you will find it can be lonely. If you have forgotten your purpose and started to climb just for the money or recognition, it will most definitely be lonely.

Master climbers form a small team to climb with them. This should include a mentor or two ahead of you for guidance. Alongside you, you'll need to enlist partners to assist with your weaknesses so you can focus on your strengths. As discussed, wildly creative types will probably need to outsource bookkeeping and financial planning, for example. Visionary leaders often need help with execution and administration. Trusted team members, along with your significant other, best friends, or family will be the ones to push you up that final ledge when you start to slip. Remember this climbing team will be small, it is not the same as your tribe. It is vital that you think through who you are climbing for, your tribe, and be careful about who you are climbing with, your team. If a couple years from now you look to your left or right and find you don't like who you see on your team, perhaps it's time for a course correction.

Leading the Way

This is not necessarily a book about leadership, but I'm sure most of you reading it want to be a leader. You want to reach the hilltop of influence. You may glamorize the idea of being an "expert" in your field, hiring a personal assistant, or having college kids practically beg to be your intern. Well, what you'll learn when you find a mentor to follow, or better yet when you start to ascend, is that, as Sam Cummings said, "The higher you climb on the mountain, the harder the wind blows."

When you are out in front, you're the first to feel the wind, there's no barrier of warm bodies for you. When you are leading the way and you come to a rickety wooden bridge that resembles the only way out of the Temple of Doom, you are Indiana Jones. You have to make the decision to cross. Even if you ask the tribe for feedback, even if you make it a vote, they look to you and the decision lies with you. Leadership is a giant topic that has been covered in many books. I recommend anything by John C. Maxwell or Stephen Covey for starters. But you are going solo, which means you are primarily leading yourself, your family, and a handful of colleagues. Just remember that those who climb to the top are looked up to, followed, and revered. This may mean employees or this could simply mean you're leading your spouse and kids. With a tribe comes great joy and fulfillment, but also great responsibility. Prepare yourself for both. If you don't add value to your tribe, as well as your climbing team, if you are not loving them, sharing with them, and investing in them, you probably won't continue uphill for long. Or even worse, you'll end up at the top shouting "Guys! Wow! Look at this view!" and you'll turn around and everyone will be gone. What a sad thought to get there and have no one to share your joy with!

Stay Disciplined

So, you've finally reached some landmarks and now you're leading in your industry and have a small team of all-stars around you. What next? Well, remember that the minute you stop climbing you start you can start slipping. I love Zig's famous quote that reads, "People often say that motivation doesn't last. Well, neither does bathing — that's why we recommend it daily."

We have addressed that you'll have to take breaks to find inspiration and assess your path. But, reaching a hilltop may tempt some to get complacent. Once you finally start your business or launch your product, you might be tempted to let your personal brand slide. It seems harmless; after all you just reached the top of an important hill!

Well, yes, but it's a hill. Remember you're aiming for 65, not 35. I can think of multiple people right now who have made it into a job they love so they have put their dreams on hold and let their Awesome File become outdated. A job once loved can become a job truly dreaded as soon as a teammate is hired or fired. We have all seen one terrible client or one project from hell send a business into a tailspin. Entrepreneurs often "keep their heads down" and focus on the work, but if you need to prepare for another big opportunity a few months or years from now, it will be much harder to rework your entire website that you haven't touched since launching! Stay committed to your calendar alerts and daily climbing practices from Chapters 5 and 6. Take time to stop and think about new directions and to reflect again like you did at the base of this particular hill.

Keep Learning

Part of discipline is to remember that if you're learning you're climbing and if you're climbing you're learning. The two go hand in hand. Since we just covered that you're not going to let yourself get complacent, we know that when you reach a landmark on your journey, you will immediately start looking ahead. What does the next phase of the journey hold? What classes can you take? What books can you read about your next challenge? As you ascend, things may get a bit scary. Success can be scary. It's been said that having all of your dreams come true before your eyes can be as startling as failure. A bigger crowd may be watching below. There may be more pressure at such a high altitude. Don't let fear creep in now! Just like when you began, start with the next few steps. Find clarity for your very next move and start heading that way. Find a mentor who can help to guide you if you haven't already. Find new teammates that will keep you on your toes. Find conferences that you can attend. I'm always amazed to read that successful people, the kind with *New York Times* best selling books and over 300,000 blog subscribers, still work with coaches and go to seminars. You would think that once they become a keynote speaker, they'd then be too legit to ever go to a conference again as an attendee, but they do. And, you will too, because you want to reach your mountaintop. Take some time to research books you want to read, classes you want to take, and conferences you want to attend. Write them down and set reminders for yourself so you stay on track!

Stay Inspired

If you had a college experience like mine, even your alarm clock was downright inspirational back then. In that time of life, creativity oozed out of everyone and everything. Each day was full of possibility. When I go back to the University of Oklahoma campus to speak or for football games — Boomer Sooner! — I still get all tingly. But, after college we entered the real world and went into shock. It happened to all of us. It almost seems as though each year in the workforce adds a layer of smog you have to clear through to find the sun that is inspiration. Thirty years of "make the logo bigger" will crush anyone's spirits. When you're on your 20th rewrite or tenth round of prototypes from the manufacturer, you may or may not want to die. We've all been there. Parts of the climb will take everything you've got. When that happens, it's time to refill your tank so you can keep climbing.

Just like Zig says we have to motivate daily, Jack London says "You can't wait for inspiration, you have to go after it with a club." Inspiration is waiting for you. It's online, it's outside, it's at the coffee shop. It's at that new art gallery. It's over coffee with the friend you haven't seen in a while. Think back to why you started your journey in the first place. Give yourself a pat on the back for how far you've come. **It's no one else's job to keep you inspired.** Climbers go find inspiration and keep finding it. Remind yourself again of activities that leave you feeling inspired on the worksheet provided on page xxxiv.

Anticipate Adversity

Part of staying inspired is making sure you have enough inspiration and motivation to get you through valleys, or valley-inducing circumstances. For example, what if you lose a huge client or purchase order? What if you suddenly get some hateful comments online about your blog or business? Everything you have gone through in this book actually encompasses all the things to keep you going, but it's a lot to think through when you're in the trenches. So, today we are going to designate a place in our home that we see everyday. A mirror, desktop background, bulletin board, or space of wall in the office or kitchen, whatever works for you. There, let's post the following things:

Revised Mission Statement

Try and get your mission statement down into five or six words. You could list five or six nouns "Writer. Inspirer. Mother." etc. More powerful, however, is to create an identity statement that starts with "I am" or "I (verb)." For myself, I could use "I inspire greatness in others." or "I empower solopreneurs towards greatness." Not only does this serve as a powerful elevator pitch, if you have not launched yet, it serves as an affirmation every time you say it! I *am* pursuing my dreams. I *will* do what I love one day. Isn't that empowering? Plus, the vehicle for your mission within that statement can change, but the mission remains the same. For example, you may launch a product now and a whole business platform later, or maybe an e-book now, an online course on the subject later. Get your statement as short as possible, print it or write it and post it!

A Face and a Name

We discussed already that you need to know who you're climbing for and how you're enriching the world with your passions and gifts. But, on a stormy day when you're about to fall off a cliff, it might be too easy to say "Forget you guys, I'm going back down to that safe spot I saw!" However, if you put a face and a name to your audience, it's harder to say no to that specific person that needs you. For example, Jenny really needs you to put out that funny illustration series for single women. She's facing depression, feeling alone, in need of encouragement and *today* might be the day she stumbles upon your Pinterest board or website. *Today* might be the end of the rope for her and your funny, uplifting illustrations might be the one thing that keeps her from losing it. The thing that makes her feel like someone in the world "gets" her! How can you say no to Jenny? How can you quit today when Jenny is in such a dark place without you? The answer is you can't. Which is precisely why you're going to get a fake image off of the Internet, print it out and put "JENNY" underneath her face, and write a few things about her and why she desperately needs what only you can give.

In addition to Jenny, you are also probably climbing for your family. I want to be an example to my daughter; I want to provide income for my family; I want to be able to support my husband's dreams. So, I will post a photo of them as well. Whoever else keeps you motivated to keep going, post their photo as well. What a powerful difference this will make when we want to give up!

Fellow Climbers

We've already covered the importance of finding a mentor and accountability partner. Eventually, you'll have a team that helps you either as volunteers or employees. Once you have found them, post their photos as well. For mentors and accountability partners, it might be a good idea to also post what you've agreed upon together; "Monthly calls or weekly Skype sessions that cover three goals." For employees or team members, you may want to post a photo of them with their family or spouse, a reminder that you are affecting a person's family and livelihood!

List the Benefits

We already know *why* we are climbing at all, our mission and contribution to the world, and *who* we are climbing for. We've put a face and name with them so we have a harder time giving up. But, all of the things listed so far have been outward, and on the frontend. Now it's time to remember the benefits you personally will have after having have accomplished your dream. Will you finally be able to quit your soul-sucking job? Finally be out of debt? Feel a sense of overwhelming relief or amazing accomplishment? Seeing the gold at the rainbow posted where you can see it everyday will remind you of just how sweet the view from the top is going to be! Can't stop climbing or you'll miss it! Use the checklist and worksheet at the end of this chapter to make sure you have everything important posted all in one spot that you see daily.

Revise Regularly

Even though my journey so far has been, well, a crazy whirlwind, I still feel like I am fortunate to have had so many course corrections relatively early on. Just like starting is important, so is revising. Not everyone plans what they'll be when they are young and ends up, or stays in, that field their entire career. According to a 2013 report from the Federal Reserve Bank of New York, only 23 percent of college grads have jobs related to their degrees. Ninety-one percent of the workforce born between 1977-1997 expected to stay in a job for less than three years, according to the Future Workplace "Multiple Generations @ Work" survey. That adds up to 15 to 20 jobs over the course of their working lives, and that was back in '97! If you are watching the trail signs; where you are spending your time, your likes and dislikes, your strengths and weaknesses, you will have new revelations along your journey. Expect them. Embrace them. Each course correction gets you either closer to your end goal or at least away from a path that wasn't right for you. With each revision, your path gets clearer.

The truly great never reach the top. The highest they've been is just the highest they've been so far. There are always more people to reach with their message and mission. Master climbers keep on keeping on because they've chosen a climb and a peak that they love. However, don't confuse a purpose-driven passion-filled climb with a happy, easy life. Fulfillment is its own kind of happiness, and it usually doesn't come easily. Every day of the climb will not be sunny, clear and filled with sweet the sounds of nature. Some days you'll be stuck in a torrential downpour of life. Sometimes you'll step in deer droppings. Some days you'll get stuck in a bear trap. Sometimes it'll be as hot as the Sahara and you'd be thirsty for inspiration and none will come. You'll have to climb anyway. You'll have to look at your bulletin board and remember there is someone out there somewhere who needs what only you can offer them! If you think about it, life will throw you great days and terrible days either way — how much easier to push through a horrible day when you're working on your dream instead of wandering aimlessly!

CONCLUSION
Now is Your Time

> "Every mountain top is within reach if you just keep climbing."
> *Barry Finlay*

James the carpenter went through this book, walked out of his oil and gas job and into his dream. Lucy combined her bookkeeping skills and her passion for dance and opened her own studio. Ben launched three more apps, the last of which went on to make him a million dollars and helps thousands of users manage their finances. Sally picked up her pen in the evenings after her kids went to sleep and started a blog. That blog turned into a book, which led her out of the church job she had back in Shouldland. Ginger the brainiac finally launched her products into the marketplace, and gets giddy seeing her work on the shelves of local retail stores. Sam took the time to really evaluate his design career, and soon realized his true passion was web design. He launched as a freelance web designer and now makes more money because his passion fuels him to work harder and better than ever before. Jane, ordinary and talentless, realized that her heart for others and work experience set her up to start her own non-profit which went on to help thousands of families with disabled children.

    Except, of course, those characters aren't real. But, you are. Now is your time! What will you launch? What will you start? How many lives will you touch? How will your life change? How will you radically elevate your family, your community? I ask again, can you smell the fresh air? Can you see the peaks on the horizon? You have your tools now, you've mapped your course, you are ready and excited for the climb ahead. You know that as you draw closer to the mountain, the massive height of your solopreneurial dreams becomes a reality. Even if your legs are shaky and your palms are sweaty, keep going. Even if you have no tribe at the base with you, start anyway. Even if a couple Negative Nancies managed to sneak into your backpack, march onward. Even if you slip a few times, or change your course often. Even if you develop a fear of heights. Even if your feet grow sore. Even if your load becomes heavy. The view from the top, the breathtaking expanse of a passion-filled life, the brightness of the sun above those clouds of meaninglessness and longing, that view is waiting for you. The world needs you to see it. You deserve to see it. Your glorious peak awaits, so keep climbing!

ABOUT THE AUTHOR

Kelsey Humphreys is an emerging authority on the subjects of branding, marketing, entrepreneurship and personal development. After starting her career as a graphic designer, her passion for those subjects led her to become the Associate Creative Director at one of Oklahoma's largest advertising agencies. She then landed and international client and was able to quit her dream job for her dream; starting her own business.

She is one of the most driven entrepreneurs you'll ever meet, but she'll be the first to tell you, all that drive wasn't always pointed in the right direction. Before focusing on her design career, her entrepreneurial journey included a few course corrections; from wanting to be the next big pop star, a short stint with MLM, an Etsy shop and lifestyle blog, and even moving to a tiny lake town in Arkansas to run the family marina. Now she speaks, consults, coaches, and writes to help other multi-passionate entrepreneurs avoid her mistakes and launch a solo business they'll truly love.

Humphreys still loves the stage, and has captivated crowds ranging from 70 to 19,000. She creates engaging and informative presentations about personal development and entrepreneurship. To have her present at your event, check her availability at kelseyhumphreys.com/speaking

Humphreys lives in Oklahoma City, Oklahoma with her high school sweetheart husband, their daughter, and two feisty dogs. Connect with her and let her know what you thought of the book:

Blog: kelseyhumphreys.com
Facebook.com/KelseyHumphreys
Twitter.com/KelseyHumphreys
Youtube.com/KelseyHumphreys

GO SOLO ACTION GUIDE

🔥 FIND your PASSION ⊕ FOCUS your EFFORT ◎ FULFILL your PURPOSE

Download a separate, printable PDF of this guide at timetogosolo.com!

FULFILL your PURPOSE

FOCUS your EFFORT

FIND your PASSION

MADE FOR MORE
You've been given traits and talents as unique as your DNA, and the world needs what you have to offer!

What are your strengths and your best personality traits?
List everything that's good about yourself. Don't be bashful, list all of it!

_____
_____
_____
_____
_____

What are your skills and talents?
This could be anything from drawing cartoons to being able to understand and edit down very complex issues and teach them to others. List anything you're really good at.

_____
_____
_____
_____
_____

What do others say you are so "gifted" at? What do others admire about you?
This could be something obvious like singing to something not so obvious like being a great listener.

_____
_____
_____
_____
_____

Is there anything that you've ever felt "born to do?" This can include all old and new dreams, **even from childhood.**

_____
_____
_____
_____
_____

If you had all the money in the world and no responsibilities what would you do?

_____
_____
_____
_____
_____

What do you feel is your mission or message to others?
If you don't have one yet that's okay, start brainstorming about what's important to you. This could be very personal, for example, to be the best mom you can be, or very broad, like ending world hunger.

_____
_____
_____
_____
_____
_____
_____

FULFILL your PURPOSE
FOCUS your EFFORT
FIND your PASSION

YOUR PEAK
To arrive at your dream destination, and to make a plan to get there, you first need to determine where it is.

When I peak in life, I will have "made it" because

_____
_____
_____

My ideal business/source of income/work that matters would be:

_____
_____

My lifestyle will be (married? kids? mansion? free time? private jet? free to travel often? Where will you live? Work from home or skyscraper office?):

_____
_____
_____
_____
_____

My dream day includes (describe from morning to night):

_____
_____
_____
_____

My typical weekend will be spent:

_____
_____
_____

When you look back on your life, what do you think you will most regret NOT doing?

_____
_____
_____
_____

What do you want to be remembered for?

_____
_____
_____
_____
_____
_____
_____
_____

Grab some paper or open a document and write out your obituary.

YOUR CLIMB

When you choose a destination, you really choose a journey. Think through the daily details of achieving your dream.

Over the last year, when have you been happiest?

_____

_____

Over the last year, when have you been most fulfilled?

_____

_____

Why did you think you felt happiest and fulfilled then?

_____

_____

What could you enjoy doing every single day, forever?

_____

_____

What are all of the aspects of your current job/career that you enjoy? _____

_____

_____

What are all of the aspects of your hobbies that you enjoy?

_____

_____

_____

What do you hate about your career, job, or day to day obligations? What do you put off as long as possible?

_____

_____

_____

Why do you hate those things?

_____

_____

_____

What tasks or challenges do you do best? What gets you most excited?

_____

_____

_____

Why are those tasks and challenges fulfilling and exciting?

_____

_____

_____

FULFILL your PURPOSE

What have you spent most of your obligation-free time doing in the past year? _____
_____
_____

FOCUS your EFFORT

What do you most enjoy reading, watching, listening to, learning about? _____
_____
_____
_____

FIND your PASSION

What inspires you most?
_____
_____
_____

Why do you think that inspires you?
_____
_____
_____

CLARIFY YOUR WHY
When the climbing gets tough, the tough carry on because they remember why they're climbing.

Who Are You Climbing For?
Besides building a business to support your family or community, how does your solo dream help others? Who does it help most? Describe your target client or customer, your tribe, in great detail. If you invented a new high tech vacuum your tribe would include medium to high income families, primarily mothers.

Write A Personal Mission Statement

Think through your goals, dreams, and core values. Look for repeated words and themes throughout your answers. Then go to **http://www.franklincovey.com/ and use the FREE online mission statement builder**. This tool will generate a very long but accurate mission statement. Try and edit that down to a couple paragraphs. Write them below.

FULFILL your PURPOSE

FOCUS your EFFORT

FIND your PASSION

ADD VALUE WHERE YOU ARE
Opportunity favors the prepared. Find ways to practice excellence now in order to be ready for going solo later.

How can you be more helpful to your leaders? (If you don't know the answer, ask them and write it here!)

_____

_____

_____

How can you be more helpful to your team mates or those you lead? (If you don't know the answer, ask them and write it here!)

_____

_____

_____

How can you be more resourceful and more independent on your projects?

_____

_____

_____

FULFILL your PURPOSE

How can you help the reputation or external image of the company? (Networking? Blogging? Speaking? Volunteering?)

_____
_____
_____
_____

FOCUS your EFFORT

How can you improve internal morale and communication?

_____
_____
_____
_____

FIND your PASSION

What are some holes in your company that you could fill? Launch an internship program? Reorganize internal reports or archives? Finish a big internal project that's been on the back burner forever? Start a company blog or Pinterest account?

_____
_____
_____
_____

What have you learned from your current job? What lessons will help you when you go solo, for example, good/bad things leaders have done, projects that have been huge successes or failures, etc?

_____
_____
_____
_____

AWESOME FILE

Use this checklist to make sure you are ready for your Big One when the time comes!

Last 3 to 6 months of projects including the following for EACH project (if applicable)

- [ ] Before image, statistics
- [ ] After image, statistics
- [ ] Brief synopsis of how you rocked it
- [ ] Charts or stats on how your project helped the client (think increased visibility, increased sales) or your company (better client/partner relationship, tackling new ground that your company hadn't tried before, etc)
- [ ] Client/boss/team testimonials, emails, chats

List the following over the last 3-6 months (add any graphics, screenshots, or photos applicable)

- [ ] Awards won
- [ ] Features (on other websites, as an expert on blogs, etc)
- [ ] Ways you have helped internal morale, communications, team building, company vision/mission etc.

- [ ] I have updated my website and online portfolios with everything from the last 3 months (employer permitting).
- [ ] I have updated my calendar alerts to remind me to update my file and portfolios again in 3 months.

FULFILL your PURPOSE | FOCUS your EFFORT | FIND your PASSION

PERSONAL BRANDING
It's time to invest in yourself! Use these pages to make it easy for your Big One to find you.

Write An Objective Statement

From your mission statement, create a personal objective statement to use on your website. This statement should introduce in one sentence who you are and what you want to be doing (or are doing if you've already started). **Remember this is not a resume statement of where you've been, it's an objective state of where you're headed.** A good formula is to include an {action}, for {a target audience} that you do in order to {how do you add value target audience}.

For example, Hi I'm James and I am saving sophisticated consumers {audience} from mundane cookie-cutter decor {value} by creating custom beautiful, unique, high quality furniture pieces {action}.

_____
_____
_____
_____
_____
_____
_____
_____

For your personal brand you may want to create a logo. If so, find a professional and give them color, pattern, and texture guidelines that match your personality and objectives. While you want to stay true to yourself, you also want to attract your Big One. If your target audience is men in their 40's you should think about what would appeal to them. If your big one is an innovative tech venture capitalist, you want to make sure your branding would appeal to them as opposed to a more traditional, conservative design and color pallet. The designer can also create your personal business cards with a condensed version of your objective or mission statement prominently displayed.

PERSONAL BRANDING CHECKLIST

- [ ] Purchased yourname.com or similar professional personal URL that matches your mission statement.
- [ ] Set up professional personal email account
- [ ] Have set up a website using Wordpress or Squarespace, etc
- [ ] Have created an objective statement
- [ ] Have made sure objective is clearly visible on website
- [ ] Have added relevant resume information
- [ ] Have added your work examples, reports or case studies
- [ ] Have added testimonials from clients, colleagues, teachers, parents, whatever is applicable.
- [ ] Have written a social media bio for yourself that matches your objective statement.
- [ ] Have taken an updated, professional headshot
- [ ] Have updated bio, profile headshot, and personal URL on all social media accounts
- [ ] Have set a calendar alert on your phone or via email that reminds you to update your website regularly

PERSONAL MARKETING

If done intentionally, the way you share, snap, post and tweet can help your Big One find you.

Create Content Categories For Your Social Sharing

James the carpenter, for example, would have personal, his work, carpentry teaching/tips, and interior design as his categories. Remember to use categories that line up with your objective and allow you to post things that will appeal to your Big One and make it easier for them to find you.

Category 1 _____

Category 2 _____

Category 3 _____

Category 4 Personal (you can't successfully do social without sharing personal posts and personality)

Next, think through each social media platform and post category percentages. Your blog content may be more personal than what you post to Facebook. Twitter and LinkedIn are much less personal platforms than Pinterest and Instagram, etc.

Platform _____	Platform _____
_____ ____%	_____ ____%
_____ ____%	_____ ____%
_____ ____%	_____ ____%
_____ ____%	_____ ____%

Platform _____		Platform _____

_____ ____%		_____ ____%
_____ ____%		_____ ____%
_____ ____%		_____ ____%
_____ ____%		_____ ____%

Platform _____		Platform _____

_____ ____%		_____ ____%
_____ ____%		_____ ____%
_____ ____%		_____ ____%
_____ ____%		_____ ____%

- [ ] Have set up calendar alerts to remind you to research competitors, follow new people on social media profiles, and update social photo galleries, Pinterest boards, etc.

FULFILL your PURPOSE
FOCUS your EFFORT
FIND your PASSION

SETTING YOUR PACE
Take your time, but take it strategically. Don't feel like you have to fill out the whole page, just start, and **use pencil.**

Sum up what you hope to have accomplished late in life?
(This may be by 50, 60 or 80 depending on your dreams and goals.)

_____
_____
_____
_____

How can you start small now to work your way towards the goals above? For example if your end goal is to write for The New York Times, you could immediately pitch your writing to local newspapers or regional magazines.

_____
_____
_____
_____

Now break your goals up into chunks of time:

Achieved 1 year from now   Action steps to make this happen

_____   • _____
_____   • _____
_____   • _____
_____   • _____

Look at the goals above and choose a reasonable goal date to quit your job and go solo full time: _____

5 years from now

_____

_____

_____

_____

Action steps to make this happen

- _____
- _____
- _____
- _____

10-20 years from now

_____

_____

_____

_____

Action steps to make this happen

- _____
- _____
- _____
- _____

Look at all you want to do! That's awesome. But stop and think through habits right now that you know are holding you back.

_____

_____

_____

_____

Action steps to stop these habits

- _____
- _____
- _____
- _____

☐ Have downloaded and printed or purchased a planner to keep you on track each day, week and month.

☐ Have exercised the Return on Investment concept for my time and started to change my habits.

☐ Have figured out my sweet spot for productivity at work and at home to best use that time.

FELLOW CLIMBERS
We become like those we spend the most time with - choose wisely.

FULFILL your PURPOSE

Identify 2-4 people that you could approach about becoming your mentor, set a deadline for yourself.

_____
_____
_____

FOCUS your EFFORT

I will have a mentor by _____

Identify fellow go-getters who inspire you and why. Find one to be your accountability partner. These are the people you want to surround yourself with!

_____
_____
_____

FIND your PASSION

I will have an accountability partner by _____

Identify Negative Nancies in your life. Limit your time with these folks. Haters on this list? Remove them from your life if possible!

_____
_____
_____

Identify people you can invest in and encourage. There are people in your life who look up to you, team mates, employees, spouse, children. Find ways to pump others up!

_____
_____

Once you go solo, it can get lonely. Start to brainstorm other solo acts in town that you could meet with for coffee or brainstorming meetings in order to keep yourself from going stir crazy

RESEARCH & RECON
Before you launch it's important to research your market, competition, and target audience.

Inspiration: Who is doing your mission well, **both** locally and online? List a few people you can study and learn from.

_____
_____
_____
_____

What things are the people listed above doing well? Not doing well?

_____
_____
_____

What topics do they cover in their content? How often do they update their blog/videos/content?

_____
_____
_____

What products and services do they sell? What is their business model?

_____
_____
_____

What kind of culture/lifestyle do they create/promote? How do they use social media?

How can you differentiate yourself from them?

Who are they trying to reach? How is your target audience different from theirs? Can you focus in on a more specific group?

Think about the questions and problems your target client or customer faces. What is missing in the solutions from your competitors? What holes can you fill?

Now focus on your target customer or client. Get specific and even create a fake name and "profile" for them. Age? Gender? Ethnicity? Where do they shop, eat, hangout? What are they passionate about? What do they hate/love? Are they on Facebook, Instagram? What other brands do they like? What do they struggle with? What do they research on the Internet?

GET DOWN TO BUSINESS

You've started gaining momentum and you are getting close to breaking out on your own. Time to make a plan.

Finances: The biggest reason we all hesitate going solo. Let's figure out what you'll need below.

Amount of monthly income you need to feel comfortable: _____(i)

Your hourly rate, or average amount of income per product: _____(h)

Your monthly expenses total: _____(e)

Obviously, $h(\text{\# of hours or products}) = i$ So, divide your income by the hours or product to see just how much you'll need to produce per month.

Profit goal for the first year: _____ divided by 12 = _____(p)

So $i - e = p$

Reduce Old Expenses
Can you remove or reduce any of your monthly expenses? Buy generic? Cancel cable? You can add luxuries back when you are living your dreams!

Plan for New Expenses
What expenses will be added when you go solo, for example losing your company gas card, paying for insurance, working extra to give yourself sick days and vacation days etc.

What start up expenses will you incur? Filing as an LLC, Will you need to purchase equipment, software licenses, classes, etc.? Organizational fees? Will you need to rent office space if you can't work from home?

When you go solo, you have to wear all the hats. What will you need to outsource? Think through your strengths and weaknesses from the previous exercises. It may be more cost effective to pay a skilled vendor for one hour of their time versus ten hours trying to figure some aspects of business out yourself!

Think through the questions above to get a new total for e.

FULFILL your PURPOSE • FOCUS your EFFORT • FIND your PASSION

Next figure out a few revenue stream ideas, to increase *i* without having to kill yourself on *h*. Fill out what you could do in each stream:

Add ons, Upgrades, Packages (How can you enhance the offerings you already have? Combo packages? New editions? Updgrade fees?)

___

Informational Products (how-to e-book or physical book, guide, webinars, online courses, recorded courses as a DVD set or set that you can purchase and stream anytime):

___

Tools (tutorials, documents, templates):

___

Speaking (talking about what you do):

___

Consulting (for businesses) or **Coaching** (one-on-one for people, or groups of people):

___

xxvi

Events (workshops, live conference or mastermind with other experts):

_____
_____
_____

Affiliate Products (items relevant to your business that you recommend and sell through amazon, earning a commission):

_____
_____
_____

A paid App? Monthly Subscription websites? **Other Ideas?**

_____
_____
_____
_____
_____
_____

Which revenue streams could you start **before quitting** your day job?

_____
_____
_____

FULFILL your PURPOSE

REBRAND
As you start to get close to launching, you can rework your personal branding to fit your new business!

FOCUS your EFFORT

Take your previous personal mission & objective statement and re-purpose it for your business. The carpenter, James, could take his personal statement: "Hi I'm James and I am saving sophisticated consumers {audience} from mundane cookie-cutter decor {value} by creating custom beautiful, unique, high quality furniture pieces {action}." His Business mission could read: "Creating hand-crafted custom furniture and carpentry for the sophisticated consumer."

FIND your PASSION

From your mission statement, create a short slogan to use on your marketing materials, remember it cannot just be catchy, it needs to also accurately represent your mission: James slogan could read: "Sophisticated hand-crafted Carpentry." or if his business name is Lastname Carpentry, his slogan could read "Quality, Handcrafted."

For your marketing materials, in addition to your slogan, have a few positioning statements, highlighting how you fill the holes in the market you listed on the previous worksheet. Focus on the benefit of working with you or purchasing from you. "Buy X from me, and you get Y."

MARKETING MAGIC
Go from starting to striving much faster with the use of strategic marketing

Content: Take the categories from your personal branding and make a schedule for posting content. Figure out what you want to post and when. Brainstorm below and then create a calendar for yourself on your computer, phone or planner. For a great guide to content marketing check out the free guide offered by QuickSprout.

Kinds of Content: What kinds of things will you be able to post consistently and enjoy creating each week? Remember your strengths! If you are not good on camera don't try to make videos, etc. Also consider what your target audience prefers to consume, editorial blog posts? how-to videos? before and after images?

_____

_____

_____

_____

Schedule: Do not post the same content category everyday, or all content categories everyday. Focus on the social media platforms that your target audience spends time on. For example if your target audience is above 55, they are probably not on Pinterest or Instagram, etc.

Monday _____

Tuesday _____

Wednesday _____

Thursday _____

Friday _____

Saturday _____

Sunday _____

xxx

Culture: Go beyond your services and products to create a culture or promote a lifestyle. Describe your brand culture below:

_____
_____
_____
_____

How can you infuse the values, culture and lifestyle into your categories? How can you sprinkle in your personality and a bit of your personal life?

Category : _____

_____
_____

Category : _____

_____
_____

Category : _____

_____
_____

Category : _____

_____
_____

Category : _____

_____
_____

☐ Have set up a calendar for what content to post and when.

FULFILL your PURPOSE

START WHERE YOU ARE
Review the Setting Your Pace worksheet. What can you start now? Set some short term deadlines for yourself.

FOCUS your EFFORT

Tasks for today/this week: Deadline

_____   _____
_____   _____
_____   _____
_____   _____
_____   _____

FIND your PASSION

Tasks for this month:

_____   _____
_____   _____
_____   _____
_____   _____
_____   _____
_____   _____

Next month:

_____   _____
_____   _____
_____   _____
_____   _____

☐ Set a realistic schedule to make sure you set aside time each week, put schedule in your digital or written calendar, or even set reminder alarms for yourself.

START WITH WHAT YOU HAVE
Identify time, tools, and ideas that you already have available.

Available time I can use right now towards launching my business: Could you record voice memos of ideas or to-dos in your phone on your drive to work? Wake up a few hours earlier or stay up a few hours later? Use your lunch breaks, etc.

_____

_____

_____

_____

_____

Tools I have or can afford to purchase right now to help my dream become a reality sooner. If you want to be a writer, you can start a blog right away, if you want to be a full-time photographer you have your current camera and you could buy some new Photoshop actions or affordable online courses. If you want to be a consultant you could consult for a few friends for free in order to build case studies. Get creative!

_____

_____

_____

_____

_____

_____

_____

KEEP LEARNING, STAY INSPIRED

Write out ideas for educational and inspirational materials now so you have ammunition against complacency later.

FULFILL your PURPOSE · FOCUS your EFFORT · FIND your PASSION

Activities that leave you feeling inspired:

_____
_____
_____

Books you want or need to read:

_____
_____
_____
_____
_____

Set a hard goal to read _____ books a month.

Classes or conferences you want or need to attend:

_____
_____
_____
_____
_____

☐ Set up calendar alerts for enrollment deadlines.

KEEP YOUR EYE ON THE PRIZE

Print and/or write out the important things about your climb and post them where you can see them daily!

Condense your mission statement into 5 or 6 "I am" or "I do" statement. _____

_____

_____

Put a face, name and story on WHO needs what you can only offer rather than just "students" or "moms." _____

_____

_____

_____

Remember the benefits, the view from the top! What will you have after having achieved your dreams and goals? ___

_____

_____

_____

I have posted the following things where I can see them every day:

- [ ] Condensed Mission Statement
- [ ] Face/Name/Story of WHO I want to help
- [ ] Faces of family members I am climbing for
- [ ] Face/Name/Commitment with Mentor
- [ ] Face/Name/Commitment with Accountability Partner
- [ ] List or Photos of the BENEFITS I'll have after achieving my goals

Made in the USA
Charleston, SC
11 July 2016